ArtScroll Judaica Classics®

Rabbi Nosson Scherman / Rabbi Meir Zlotowitz

General Editors

סֵפֶר יוֹנָה

YONAH

"Journey of the Soul"

An allegorical commentary adapted from

The Vilna Gaon's
Aderes Eliyahu

The
Book of

by
Rabbi Moshe Schapiro

Published by
Mesorah Publications, ltd

FIRST EDITION
First Impression . . . August 1997

Published and Distributed by
MESORAH PUBLICATIONS, Ltd.
4401 Second Avenue
Brooklyn, New York 11232

Distributed in Europe by
J. LEHMANN HEBREW BOOKSELLERS
20 Cambridge Terrace
Gateshead, Tyne and Wear
England NE8 1RP

Distributed in Israel by
SIFRIATI / A. GITLER—BOOKS
10 Hashomer Street
Bnei Brak 51361

Distributed in Australia & New Zealand by
GOLDS BOOK & GIFT CO.
36 William Street
Balaclava 3183, Vic., Australia

Distributed in South Africa by
KOLLEL BOOKSHOP
22 Muller Street
Yeoville 2198, Johannesburg, South Africa

ARTSCROLL JUDAICA CLASSICS®
YONAH — Journey of the Soul
© Copyright 1997, by MESORAH PUBLICATIONS, Ltd.
4401 Second Avenue / Brooklyn, N.Y. 11232 / (718) 921-9000

ISBN:
1-57819-160-2 (hard cover)
1-57819-161-0 (paperback)

Typography by CompuScribe at ArtScroll Studios, Ltd.
4401 Second Avenue / Brooklyn, N.Y. 11232 / (718) 921-9000

Printed in the United States of America by Edison Lithographing and Printing Corp.
Bound by Sefercraft Inc., Quality Bookbinders, Brooklyn, N.Y.

The Book of
Yonah

The Hebrew text of *Aderes Eliyahu* on *Yona*,
from which this commentary was adapted,
appears as an appendix to this volume

๛ *Introduction*

In addition to its literal meaning, the story of Jonah can be understood on a deeper level as an analogy to the sojourn of the *neshamah* (human soul) in this world. Jonah the Prophet represents man's *neshamah*.

God sent Jonah to rectify the moral condition of Nineveh, but instead of fulfilling God's will, Jonah tried to escape his obligation by boarding a ship bound for a different destination. Similarly, the *neshamah* is sent to rectify the world through Torah study and *mitzvos*, but instead of fulfilling its mission, it allows itself to be deceived by the body's physical impulses. The body's ability to deceive the *neshamah* in this manner is alluded to by the name Jonah[1] — in Hebrew, the word יוֹנָה is a verbal form related to the noun הוֹנָאה, "deception."[2] This etymological link forms the basis of the correlation between Jonah the Prophet and the *neshamah*. The analogy has many facets:

Just as Jonah initially failed to carry out his mission and consequently endangered his life, so too, the *neshamah* initially fails in its mission to rectify the world and consequently brings great harm upon itself in the process.[3] And although Jonah was granted a second chance to complete his mission, he was very distressed by what he perceived as his bad fortune. The same is true of the *neshamah* — when the *neshamah* fails in its mission, it is reincarnated and given another opportunity to fulfill its mission, but like Jonah, it is greatly disturbed by the necessity of reincarnation.

It is these analogies which are elaborated upon in the commentary.[4]

---

1. *Zohar* Volume II, 199a.
2. Ibid. See *Rashi, Leviticus* 25:17. Cognates of this word also appear in *Zephaniah* 3:1; *Ezekiel* 18:7.
3. *Zohar* Volume II, 199b.
4. See commentary on verse 4:1.

א וַיְהִי דְּבַר־יהוה אֶל־יוֹנָה בֶן־אֲמִתַּי לֵאמְר:

I.

1. וַיְהִי דְּבַר ה׳ אֶל יוֹנָה — And it came to pass that the word of HASHEM came to Jonah

The Sages say that whenever the term וַיְהִי, "and it came to pass," appears in Scripture, it invariably conveys distress and hardship.[1] This verse is not an exception, although at first glance it would seem to be announcing a most joyous event — the revelation of prophecy.

The note of distress in the verse stems from the fact that the *neshamah* is sent down to this world against its will. The *Zohar* teaches that when the time comes, God commands the *neshamah* to go to a particular place in the world and enter the body of a particular individual, within which it is to fulfill His will. The *neshamah* pleads with God not to banish it from its pristine heavenly environment and force it to descend to the corporeal world, where it will become subject to worldly desires and tainted by impurity and sin. However, God insists, saying, "Since the day you were created, it was for this that you were created — to be in that world." When the *neshamah* realizes this, it descends against its will and enters the person's body.[2]

As a result of the *neshamah's* great anguish over its descent to this world, it becomes disoriented and susceptible to the enticements of physical desires. It is entangled in sin just "like a gullible dove lacking understanding"[3] unwittingly steps into a trap (the Hebrew word for "dove" is the same as the prophet's name — יוֹנָה).

There is another reason for the *neshamah's* anguish over the prospect of descending to this world: It is aware that physical desire is not the only obstacle it must overcome in order to fulfill its mission — it must also face the antagonism of the nations.

In reference to this idea, the Talmud relates the incident of Elisha, who publicly donned *tefillin* in defiance of a Roman decree prohibiting the fulfillment of this *mitzvah*. He was discovered by a Roman guard, but Elisha proceeded to remove the *tefillin* and grasp them in his hand before he was apprehended. "What do you have in your hands?" the

---

1. *Bamidbar Rabbah* 10:11.
2. *Zohar* Volume II, 96b. See also *Zohar Chadash, Parashas Noach*, s.v. תיבה איהו גופא.
3. *Midrash Hane'elam, Parashas Noach*, s.v. וירח ה׳ את ריח הניחוח. The expression "like a gullible dove lacking understanding" appears in *Hosea* 7:11.

¹**A**nd it came to pass that the word of HASHEM came to Jonah son of Amittai saying,

---

guard demanded, to which Elisha answered, "The wings of a dove [יוֹנָה]." Elisha opened his hands, and miraculously, the *tefillin* he had been holding transformed into the wings of a dove.

The Talmud explains why the *tefillin* turned into the wings of a dove, and not into some other object: "Because the Congregation of Israel is likened to a dove. . .just as wings protect the dove, so too the *mitzvos* protect the Jewish People."[1]

It is evident that the dove [יוֹנָה], which symbolizes the *neshamah*, also symbolizes the Jewish People's efforts to perform *mitzvos* in times of persecution.[2] Since the *neshamah* foresees the obstacles it will face in this world, is it any wonder that it is filled with grief at the prospect of descending to this world?

Furthermore, in reference to the verse, "My dove is in the crevice of the rock, hidden by the cliff. . .,"[3] the *Zohar*[4] states: " 'My dove' — this refers to the Congregation of Israel. Just as the dove never abandons its mate, so too, the Congregation of Israel never abandons the Holy One, Blessed is He. 'Hidden by the cliff' — this refers to Torah scholars, who are never at peace in this world," for they are constantly persecuted by their enemies.[5] It is for this reason that God calls the Jewish People "My constant dove, My perfect one [תַמָּתִי]"[6] — in reference to My constant dove, My perfect one, the Sages said,[7] "[Do not read תַמָּתִי, 'My perfect one'] but תְּאוֹמָתִי, 'My twin' — just as in the case of twins, if one of the pair has a headache, its twin also experiences pain, so too, as it were, the Holy One, Blessed is He, says, 'I am with [Israel] in distress.' "[8]

The dove is a fitting symbol for the Jewish People and the *neshamah*, since it is the only bird that does not struggle when it is about to be

---

1. *Shabbos* 49a. *Rashi* explains that unlike other birds, the dove fends off predators by striking them with its wings. The wings of the dove also protect it from the cold.

2. *Vilna Gaon's* commentary on *Shabbos* 49a, based on *Tosafos* s.v. כנפיה מגינות עליה.

3. *Song of Songs* 2:14.

4. *Zohar* Volume III, page 61a; *Shir Hashirim Rabbah* 1:15.

5. See *Zohar Chadash, Parashas Balak*, s.v. אראנו ולא עתה.

6. *Song of Songs* 6:9.

7. *Shir Hashirim Rabbah* 5:2.

8. *Psalms* 91:15.

slaughtered.[1] Like the dove, the Jewish People give up their lives without a struggle in order to sanctify the Name of God. The same can be said of the *neshamah* — it disregards its own needs and complies with God's command to descend into this corporeal world. This is the intention of the verse, "Because for Your sake we are killed all the time, we are considered as sheep for slaughter."[2] In reference to this self-sacrifice, the *Midrash* states " 'Those who love Me and observe My commandments'[3]. . . — this refers to the Jewish People, who. . .give up their lives for the *mitzvos*."[4] For this reason, the *neshamah* is called "dove" in both the first and second incarnation, regardless of whether it performs good or evil deeds. In the first incarnation it is "deceived" by the body's physical desires and is therefore called "a gullible dove lacking understanding."[5] However, if it succeeds in fulfilling its mission during its second incarnation, it earns the designation, "My constant dove, My perfect one."[6]

בֶּן אֲמִתַּי — son of Amittai

The name of Jonah's father, אֲמִתַּי, Amittai, has the same spelling as the word אֲמִתִּי, "truthful." In accordance with the understanding that Jonah symbolizes the *neshamah* and the Jewish People, the verse can be taken to mean that the *neshamah* is, in a manner of speaking, the "child" of the Truthful One, the Holy One, Blessed is He. This is also the intention of the verse, "You are *children* to HASHEM, your God. . ."[7]

לֵאמֹר – saying,

Jonah is commanded to tell the Jewish People all that God has spoken to him in order that every Jew may know why he has come to the world — to rectify himself, along with the entire world.

2. קוּם לֵךְ אֶל נִינְוֵה — Arise! Go to Nineveh,

Jonah is commanded to leave the Land of Israel and travel to a

---

1. *Midrash Hane'elam, Parashas Noach*, s.v. וירח ה׳ את ריח הניחוח.
2. *Psalms* 44:23.
3. *Exodus* 20:6.
4. *Mechilta* on *Exodus* 20:5.
5. *Hosea* 7:11; see above, page 8, footnote 3.
6. *Song of Songs* 6:9.
7. *Deuteronomy* 14:1. See also *Zohar*, Volume III, 174b.

gentile city. Similarly, there comes a time when God commands the *neshamah* to leave its abode in *Gan Eden* and descend to this world.[1]

Following this analogy, the city of Nineveh represents the corporeal world. The relationship between the city of Nineveh and this world is actually based on an etymological parity: The name Nineveh, נִינְוֶה, is similar to the Hebrew term *naveihu*, נָוֵהוּ, which means "His (i.e., God's) abode." It is understood that the term "God's abode" refers to this world, as in the passage, "May we see Him. . .upon His return to *His abode*, נָוֵהוּ."[2]

Precisely because this world is God's primary dwelling place,[3] He assigns the task of rectifying the world to no other creature than man. A human being's purpose in life is truly overwhelming — he has been entrusted with the awesome task of safeguarding the palace of the King of kings.

הָעִיר הַגְּדוֹלָה — the great city,

Man is referred to as "a little universe"[4] in the sense that he is the microcosm of all existence. As stated in the *Zohar*, "When the Holy One, Blessed is He, created man, He configured within him all the patterns of the lofty mysteries of the upper universe, as well as all the patterns of the mysteries of the lower universe — they are all engraved in man."[5] Similarly, "All that exists above and below was integrated in man,"[6] for "Man . . . encompasses all images. . .all Divine Names. . .and all the universes."[7]

Hence, man is the fulcrum of reality — his every deed, word, thought or movement has the power to either rectify or damage all of existence.[8]

---

1. *Zohar* Volume II, 96b; *Zohar Chadash, Ruth Rabbah*, s.v. נפש רוח נשמה. See also *Zohar* Volume II, 111b.

2. A phrase from the *Al Hakol* prayer recited during the *Shabbos* morning prayer service, based on *Isaiah* 52:8.

3. See *Bereishis Rabbah* 19:7 s.v עיקר שכינה בתחתונים.

4. *Raya Mehemna, Parashas Pinchas* 257b, 258a; *Tikunei Zohar, Tikun* 69.

5. *Parashas Yisro* 75b, cited in *Nefesh Hachaim* (written by *R' Chaim of Volozhin*, the *Vilna Gaon's* primary disciple), Section I, Chapter 6.

6. *Parashas Tazriya* 48a, cited in *Nefesh Hachaim*, Section I, Chapter 6.

7. *Idra Rabbah* 135a, cited in *Nefesh Hachaim*, Section I, Chapter 3.

8. *Nefesh Hachaim*, Section I, Chapter 3; *Leshem Shevo Ve'achlama*, Section I, Chapter 8.

Likewise, man is referred to as a "small city," as in the verse, "There was a small city with only a few inhabitants . . .,"[1] in reference to which the Sages said, " 'A small city' refers to the human body; 'a few inhabitants' refers to the limbs of the body."[2]

For this reason the verse appends to the city of Nineveh the description "the *great* city" — to clarify that the name "Nineveh" does not represent man, the "*small* city," but rather the "great city" — i.e., the corporeal world at large, as explained above.

וּקְרָא עָלֶיהָ — and cry out to her,

The *neshamah* is instructed to impart knowledge to "the inhabitants of the great city" — i.e., to man in this world — to induce them to resist evil temptations.

This is the deeper intention of the verse, "A voice says, 'Cry out!' and [another] replies, 'What shall I cry out?' [That] 'all flesh is like grass, and all its kindness is like the blossoms of the field. Grass withers, blossoms fade when the breath of God blows on them. Indeed, Man is like grass — grass withers and flowers fade, but the word of our God will endure forever."[3] The *Zohar* interprets the verse as follows: " 'All flesh is like grass' — all men are like grass-eating beasts; 'all its kindnesses like a blossom in the field' — all acts of kindness performed by man are motivated by selfish reasons."[4]

Clearly, the "voice" that calls out to "all flesh" is the *neshamah*.

כִּי עָלְתָה רָעָתָם לְפָנָי — for their wickedness has ascended before Me.

The Sages said, "He who fulfills a single *mitzvah* gains himself a single advocate; he who commits even a single transgression gains himself a single accuser."[5] Similarly they said, "Whoever commits a transgression in this world, the transgression grasps and walks before him on the Day of Judgment. . ."[6]

The consequences of creating an "accuser" through sin are depicted

---

1. *Ecclesiastes* 9:14.
2. *Nedarim* 32b; *Koheles Rabbah* 9:22.
3. *Isaiah* 40:6-8.
4. *Tikunei Zohar* 73b.
5. *Avos* 4:13.
6. *Avodah Zarah* 5a.

in the *Zohar*: "When a person performs a *mitzvah*, it ascends and stands before the Holy One, Blessed is He, and declares, 'I am from so-and-so, who made me!' . . . If a person commits a transgression, that transgression ascends before Him and declares, 'I am from so and so, who made me!' The Holy One, Blessed is He, then appoints it to remain there, so that He may gaze upon it and destroy the sinner."[1]

This is the intention of the verse "their wickedness has ascended before Me" — the angels that are engendered by the wicked deeds of Mankind ascend before God and demand that justice be executed against the sinners.

In reference to this, the *Zohar* also states, "When the sins of mankind grow numerous and Judgment is roused as a result of the world's sins, the Prosecutor comes and lodges accusations before the Holy One, Blessed is He, *and the Sanctuary is rendered impure*.' "[2] To understand the meaning of this statement, it is necessary to define what is meant by "the Sanctuary." The explanation is as follows:

The Holy Temple — God's Sanctuary — was a microcosmic model of the entire universe. All its edifices, storerooms, upper chambers, rooms and holy vessels were a paradigm of the Divine, representing the image, shape and form of the Holy Universes, and the structure of the components of the Divine Chariot.[3]

As mentioned above, man is a "little world" who also encompasses within him all the elements of existence — in this sense, he too is a "Sanctuary." Indeed, there are striking similarities between the layout of the Temple and human anatomy.[4]

Hence, when man sanctifies himself as required through the fulfillment of all the *mitzvos*, the Divine Presence resides within him in the same manner as it resided within the Holy Temple in Jerusalem. This is the intention of the verse, "The Sanctuary of HASHEM, the Sanctuary of HASHEM, the Sanctuary of HASHEM are they!"[5] And as the verse states,

---

1. *Zohar* Volume III, 83b; see also 214a.
2. *Zohar Chadash, Parashas Noach,* s.v. הוא ישופך ראש‎. See also *Zohar* Volume I, 54a.
3. *Nefesh Hachaim*, Section I, second note on Chapter 4.
4. Ibid.
5. *Jeremiah* 7:4.

" 'They shall make a Sanctuary for Me so that I may dwell within *them*'[1] — the sages note that the verse does not say 'so that I may dwell within *it* [i.e., the Tabernacle],' but 'within *them* — [i.e., within the Israelites].' "[2] On the other hand, when a Jew sins, he defiles the "inner Temple" that resides within him.

This is the intention of the *Zohar's* statement, "When the sins of Mankind grow numerous . . . *the Sanctuary is rendered impure*."

3. וַיָּקָם יוֹנָה לִבְרֹחַ תַּרְשִׁישָׁה מִלְפְנֵי ה' — **But Jonah arose to flee to Tarshish from before HASHEM's presence.**

Like Jonah, the *neshamah* in this world attempts to flee God's Presence — it evades its obligations and commits transgressions. As the *Zohar* states, "While in this world, man sins and thinks that he has fled from his Master."[3] Likewise it states, "Woe to the person who hides from the Holy One, Blessed is He!" For in regard to God the verse says, 'Do I not fill the heaven and the earth?'[4] How, then, can a person expect to flee from Him?[5]

This sheds new insight into why a penitent is called a *ba'al teshuvah*: The word *teshuvah* conventionally means "repentance," but translated literally, it means "to return" (the root of the word being שׁוּב, "return"). The point is that when a person knows that he is standing in God's presence, it is impossible for him to even conceive of committing a sin. Transgressions only occur when one feels distant from God, a frame of mind which deludes the individual into thinking that it is possible to evade Him.

The process of repentance, on the other hand, is essentially a realization that God's presence is everywhere; that no matter where an individual may stand, God will always be close to him. In this sense, a *ba'al teshuvah* is someone who has attempted to "flee from God," and then "returned" [שָׁב] to stand in His presence. This is the intention of the verse, "Ever since the days of your fathers, you have turned away from

---

1. *Exodus* 25:8.
2. A statement of the Sages cited by early commentators — e.g., *Alshich* on *Parashas Terumah*.
3. *Zohar* Volume II, 199a.
4. *Jeremiah* 23:24.
5. *Zohar* Volume I, 84b.

My statutes and refrained from observing them. *Return to Me* [שׁוּבוּ אֵלַי]
and I will return to you, says HASHEM, Master of Legions."[1]

תַּרְשִׁישָׁה — to Tarshish

Tarshish represents the desire to attain wealth, as is evident from the
verse, "Tarshish was your merchant because of the multitude of every
richness. With silver, iron, tin and lead they provided your wares."[2]
Similarly, the verse says, "The ships of Tarshish were your caravans for
your merchandise. Thus you were filled and made very heavy in the
heart of the seas."[3]

Following the analogy, we learn that just as Jonah "fled from God's
presence" by boarding a ship bound for Tarshish, so too, the *neshamah*
neglects to fulfill the mission for which it was brought to this world, and
instead strays after the pursuit of wealth.

מִלִּפְנֵי ה' — from before HASHEM's presence.

The verse implies that before Jonah boarded the ship to Tarshish, he
stood in God's presence. We also know from the continuation of the
story that after Jonah was cast from the ship, he repented and once again
stood in His presence. The same can be said of the *neshamah* — it stands
in God's presence before and after it is sent to this world.

As the *Zohar* states, "From the day the world was created, [the souls
of the righteous] stand before the Holy One, Blessed is He. They remain
there until the time when they must descend to earth. . . This is the
intention of the verse, 'As God, before Whom I stood, lives'[4] — the verse
does not say, 'before Whom I *stand*,' but 'before Whom I *stood*.' Afterwards, [the souls of the righteous] return to their place and ascend to
their chamber. . ."[5]

Only in the interim stage — during its sojourn in this world — does the
neshamah attempt to flee from God's presence, as in the verse,
"Cain left the presence of God."[6] Cain declared, "Behold, You have

1. *Malachi* 3:7.
2. *Ezekiel* 27:12. See *Ibn Ezra, Metzudos*.
3. Ibid, 27:25.
4. *II Kings* 5:16.
5. *Zohar* Volume III, 68b. See *Zohar* Volume I, 233b; *Zohar Chadash, Shir Hashirim*, s.v.
האדם הראשון.
6. *Genesis* 4:16.

banished me this day from the face of the earth, can I be hidden from Your presence?"[1] — the *Zohar* interprets Cain's statement to mean, "I will be hidden from Your face, *and You will not see me*."[2]

וַיֵּרֶד יָפוֹ — He went down to Jaffo

The Hebrew name of the port to which Jonah descended (יָפוֹ) is closely associated with the word יָפֶה, which means "beautiful." On a deeper level this alludes to the *neshamah's* descent to this world, for this world is also "beautiful" in the physical sense. The world's beauty stems from the Tree of Knowledge of Good and Evil, in regard to which it is written, "And HASHEM caused to sprout from the ground every tree that was *pleasing to the sight* and good for food; also the Tree of Life in the midst of the garden. . ."[3] In fact, every occurrence of the word יָפֶה in Scripture refers to physical desires, as in the verse, "And you will see among its captivity a woman who is beautiful of form (יְפַת תֹּאַר)."[4]

Just as the beauty of the Tree enticed Adam and Eve and caused them to sin, so too, the outward appeal of physical desires in this world entices the *neshamah* to sin.

וַיִּמְצָא אָנִיָּה — and found a ship

Jonah's ship symbolizes the body,[5] as the *Zohar* states, "Man goes about in this world like a ship about to break up in the ocean."[6]

The correspondence between the ship and man's physical body is evident from the double meaning of the Hebrew word אָנִיָּה — it can either mean "ship" (as in the Book of *Jonah*), or "suffering," as in the verse, "He increased within the daughter of Judah suffering and mourning (תַּאֲנִיָּה וַאֲנִיָּה)."[7]

These two meanings of the word capture the two essential aspects of Man's physical existence: It is the vessel upon which the *neshamah*

---

1. *Genesis* 4:14.
2. *Zohar* Volume I, 36b.
3. *Genesis* 2:9.56.
4. *Deuteronomy* 21:11. "The Torah only spoke in response to the Evil Inclination" (*Rashi* quoting *Sifrei*).
5. *Tikunei Zohar, Tikun* 21; *Tikun* 69.
6. *Zohar* Volume II, 199.
7. *Lamentations* 2:5.

traverses the stormy waters of this world on its voyage to the world to come, while at the same time it is a condition of interminable suffering, as it is written, "All his days are painful, and his business is a vexation. Even at night his mind has no rest . . ."[1] Similarly, the verse states, "for man is born to misery."[2]

Continuing with this analogy, the sea upon which Jonah's ship sailed represents this transient world, while the shore represents the world to come. When men set out to sea, they have no intention of staying there forever. Rather, they embark on a temporary voyage in order to earn a livelihood through trade, but they eventually return to shore with their earnings.

The same can be said of the *neshamah's* descent into the body of man — it sets sail upon the tempestuous sea that is this world in order to earn a portion in the World to Come, but it has no intention of staying here forever.

The hardships of this world are symbolized by the waves of the sea, as in the verse, "all Your breakers and Your waves passed over me,"[3] and as it is written, "waters encompassed me, to the soul [threatening my life] . . ."[4]

בָּאָה — bound for

As we have established above, Jonah's ship represents the human body. This presents a difficulty: Why does the verse use the feminine gender in connection with "ship," since the Hebrew word for "body" (גוף) is masculine?

Similarly, we may ask why all verbs used in Jonah's context are conjugated in the masculine, since it represents the *neshamah*, which in Hebrew (נשמה) carries feminine gender.

The answer is that conceptually, the *neshamah* is masculine in relation to the body. In kabbalistic terms, any entity that possesses the power of endowing some aspect of itself unto another is regarded as masculine. The entity receiving that which the "male" imparts is regarded as female.

---

1. *Ecclesiastes* 2:23.
2. *Job* 5:7.
3. *Jonah* 2:4.
4. Ibid., 2:6.

The same relationship exists between the *neshamah* and the body — conceptually, the *neshamah* is masculine in relation to the body,[1] for the *neshamah* provides guidance and animation to the body.[2] It also sustains it, as the Sages said, "Just as the Holy One Blessed is He sustains the entire universe, so too, the *neshamah* sustains the entire body."[3]

תַּרְשִׁישׁ — **Tarshish;**

As explained earlier, Jonah symbolizes the *neshamah*, Tarshish symbolizes worldly desires, and the ship represents the physical body.

In line with this deeper understanding, the verse teaches that "Jonah found a ship bound for Tarshish," meaning that the *neshamah* ("Jonah") descends into the body ("a ship") and enters a dual environment: On the one hand, the body has the potential to be a most formidable vessel through which to fulfill the Divine will, but on the other hand, the body has a predisposition for the physical desires of this world ("bound for Tarshish").

This is the deeper intention of the good[4] and evil[5] women mentioned so frequently in the Book of *Proverbs* — the "women" represent the physical body, for as explained earlier, the body is feminine in relation to the *neshamah*. In other words, when the *neshamah* utilizes the body's tremendous potential for fulfilling God's will, the body is called "a woman of valor";[6] but when the *neshamah* allows the body to pursue its natural predisposition for physical pleasures, then the body is portrayed as an evil woman.

וַיִּתֵּן שְׂכָרָהּ — **he paid its fare,**

As explained above, Jonah's act of boarding the ship bound for Tarshish is a metaphor for the *neshamah*'s descent into the body, where it either lets the body follow its natural predisposition for physical desires, or steers it towards Divine service.

When the *neshamah* chooses the former option of giving the body free rein to pursue the physical desires of this world, it perforce represses its

---

1. *Midrash Hane'elam, Lech Lecha,* s.v. לך לך מארצך.
2. See *Nefesh Hachaim*, Section I, Chapter 4.
3. *Berachos* 10a.
4. Some references to righteous women in the Book of *Proverbs* are 11:16, 12:4, 18:22, 19:14, 31:10 and 31:30.
5. Some references to evil women in the Book of *Proverbs* are 6:26, 6:32, 7:10, 9:13, 11:22, and 30:20.
6. *Proverbs* 31:10.

inherent intellectual powers. This capitulation of the *neshamah* to the body's desire for physical gratification is what the verse means by "he paid its fare" — the *neshamah* (represented by Jonah) gives in to the demands of the body and allows itself to become immersed in worldly pleasures (the ship's fare).

The concept is elaborated in *Sefer Chovos Halevavos*: "God decreed that the *neshamah* be tested within corporeal bodies. . . He instilled into the *neshamah* of humanity a desire for earthly food, and a lust for physical gratification. . . And God gave man a reward for doing these things — the sensual pleasure that accompanies these actions. And God appointed the Evil Inclination over man in order to prod him towards food and drink and physical gratification."[1]

This is also the intention of the Sages' statement, "Calculate the cost of a *mitzvah* against its reward, and the reward of a sin against its cost"[2] — the term "reward of a sin" refers to the physical pleasure which accompanies the prohibited action.

With this idea in mind, we gain a deeper insight into the Sages' statement regarding this verse: "R' Yochanan said, 'Jonah paid the fare of the entire ship.' "[3] Following our metaphoric understanding of the verse, the Sages in essence say that when the *neshamah* (represented by Jonah) capitulates to the body's desires (pays the ship's fare), all the limbs of the body ("the entire ship") derive sensual pleasure.

This also sheds light on the Sages' interpretation of the verse, "There was a small city with only a few inhabitants; and a mighty king came upon it and surrounded it, and built great siege works over it. Present in the city was a poor wise man who by his wisdom saved the town. Yet no one remembered that poor man. So I said, 'Wisdom is better than might, although a poor man's wisdom is despised and his words go unheeded.' "[4]

The Sages explain that "a small town" refers to the body, and "a few inhabitants" to the limbs. The "mighty king" is the Evil Inclination, and the "great siege works" are the transgressions it induces man to commit. The "poor wise man" is the Good Inclination."[5]

---

1. *Chovos Halevavos, Sha'ar 9, Sha'ar Haprishus*, Chapter 2.
2. *Avos* 2:1.
3. *Nedarim* 38a.
4. *Ecclesiastes* 9:14-16.
5. *Nedarim* 32b.

In light of the concepts we have outlined above, we can understand why the limbs of the body "despise" the wise counsel of the Good Inclination — it imposes limitations on them and constantly warns them of the severe consequences they will encounter in the World to Come should they succumb to their yearning for physical gratification and transgress one of God's commandments.

The Evil Inclination, on the other hand, encourages the body's limbs to immerse themselves in the pleasures of the flesh. Through its promises of instant reward, "the mighty king" gains control over the body's limbs and brings them to sin.[5]

While the Evil Inclination says to the limbs of the body, "Rejoice, young man, in your childhood . . . follow the path of your heart and the sight of your eyes,"[1] the Good Inclination warns them, "but be aware that for all these things God will call you to account."[2]

This is the deeper meaning of the term "a harlot's hire":[3] When the body strays after forbidden worldly desires, it is regarded as a harlot; the pleasure it derives from the transgression is its fee. This was the intention of King Solomon when he said, "Then behold, a women approached him, bedecked as a harlot and with siege in [her] heart."[4]

וַיֵּ֥רֶד בָּהּ — and descended into it

The neshamah must descend through many spiritual realms until it can enter the body. Its descent is akin to jumping off a high roof and plunging down a deep abyss.

4. וַֽיהוֹה – Then HASHEM

Every occurrence in Scripture of the word וַֽיהוֹה ("and HASHEM") conveys the idea that "God together with His heavenly tribunal" unanimously agree on the verdict that is to be decreed against the subject of the verse.[5] When the individual is found blameworthy, heavenly judgment turns so harsh that even the attribute of Mercy —

---

1. *Ecclesiastes* 11:9.
2. Ibid.
3. *Deuteronomy* 23:19.
4. *Proverbs* 7:10.
5. *Rashi* on *Genesis* 19:24, citing *Midrash Rabbah* 51:3.

descended into it to travel with them to Tarshish from before HASHEM's presence. ⁴ *Then HASHEM cast a mighty wind toward the sea and it became*

---

which generally speaks in defense of transgressors — consents to the demand that the most severe punishment be decreed against the sinner.[1] Jonah's attempt to evade the mission that God assigned to him elicited this stern heavenly judgment. The same can be said of the *neshamah* — when it neglects to fulfill its mission in this world, it is judged by "God together with His heavenly tribunal."

הֵטִיל רוּחַ גְּדוֹלָה — cast a mighty wind

The mighty wind that struck Jonah's ship represents the attribute of heavenly judgment. This is the spiritual entity that constantly stands before God and demands that sinners at once be given the full measure of punishment they have incurred through their transgression. It points accusingly to the sinner and screams out in indignation, "The Sanctuary has been rendered impure!" As the *Zohar* states, "The Holy One, Blessed is He, casts 'a mighty wind.' This refers to the decree which continually stands in the presence of the Holy One, Blessed is He, and demands that justice be executed against the person — this is [the wind] that came upon the ship. . ." When the prosecuting angel's accusations are finally accepted, the heavenly tribunal empowers the forces of retribution to assail the transgressor. At this point God casts the prosecuting angel down to this world, where it manifests itself as the Angel of Death. It swiftly proceeds to take the sinner's *neshamah*. The Angel of Death is called רוּחַ (wind), as the *Zohar*[2] says in reference to the verse, "Fire and hail, snow and vapor, *stormy wind* (רוּחַ סְעָרָה) fulfilling His word."[3] It is also called גְּדוֹלָה (great), for impurity is always more prominent (גָּדוֹל) than holiness, as in the verse, "Rebecca was told of the words of her older (הַגָּדֹל, literally 'great') son Esau. . ."[4] In contrast, Jacob is called "her younger (הַקָּטָן, literally 'small') son. . ."[5] This concept explains the humble behavior and diminutive bearing of

---

1. *Eitz Yosef* on *Bereishis Rabbah* 51:3.
2. *Zohar* Volume II, 1990.
3. *Zohar* Volume II 172b.
4. *Psalms* 148:8.
5. *Genesis* 27:42.

the righteous.[1] The Angel of Death takes the sinner's *neshamah* in the following manner: "At the moment of the ailing man's passing, the Angel of Death stands above the headboard of the bed with its sword drawn in its hand, and suspended [on the sword] is a drop of poison. When the ailing man sees it, he opens his mouth in astonishment, and [the Angel of Death] flings [the drop] into his mouth. It is from this drop that he dies; it is from this drop that he begins to rot; it is from this drop that his face turns yellow. . ."[2] It must be remembered that the Angel of Death is not a corporeal being, so when the Sages refer to his "sword," they are obviously speaking metaphorically. The "sword" of the Angel of Death refers to the female aspect of spiritual impurity, which is responsible for enticing man to sin. As for the "drop of poison," it refers to the impurity that enfolds the sinner in the wake of his transgression.[3] This is the same "poison" which the Serpent injected into Eve, and which introduced the concept of death to the world.[4] In fact, this is the deeper meaning of the verse, "For the lips of a forbidden woman drip honey, and her palate is smoother than oil"[5] — the "female stranger" refers to the Evil Inclination, which lures man to sin with the promise of physical pleasure.[6] The next verse says, "But her end is as bitter as wormwood, as sharp as *a double-edged sword*"[7] — one edge is this world, and the other edge is the World to Come.[8] The verse warns that should a person succumb to the enticements of the "forbidden woman," she will take his life in this world and cause him to lose his portion in the World to Come.[9] This explains why our verse uses the feminine gender for "a great wind" (רוּחַ גְּדוֹלָה) — it is the female aspect of the Evil Inclination that wields this lethal double-edged sword.

אֶל הַיָּם — **toward the sea;**

As mentioned above,[10] this world is likened to a sea, while the World to Come is likened to a shore. The metaphor can be understood more

---

1. See *Chullin* 60b; *Zohar* Volume III, 191a, 197a.
2. *Avodah Zarah* 20b.
3. See *Zohar* Volume I, 27b; Volume II, 266b, 267a.
4. *Eitz Yosef* on *Avodah Zarah* 20b.
5. *Proverbs* 5:3.
6. *Vilna Gaon's* commentary, ibid.
7. *Proverbs* 5:4.
8. *Zohar* Volume II, 266b.
9. Ibid.
10. *Vilna Gaon's* commentary on verse 1:3, s.v. וימצא אניה, "and found a ship."

clearly by pondering one of the ten questions that Alexander the Great asked the wise men of the Negev: "Where is it better to live? On the sea or on dry land?" The wise men of the Negev answered, "On dry land, for all those who embark on a sea voyage do not feel at ease until they have reached dry land."[1] There is a deeper dimension to Alexander's question than meets the eye. What he was really asking is whether spiritual existence in the World to Come is *inherently* superior to life in this world, or whether it is only superior in relation to the difficult living conditions experienced by the majority of humanity. Perhaps for a person in his situation, who ruled over the entire known world,[2] and to whom every physical desire was within easy reach, life in this world is in fact superior to life in the World to Come. Alexander's question stems from his sharing the viewpoint of a certain gentile called Bar Sheishach, who, while up to his neck in a rose bath and wallowing in sensual pleasures, asked Rava: "Is there anything like this in the World to Come?" Rava answered him, "Our [portion in the World to Come] is even better than this." [The gentile] retorted, "Nothing can possibly be better than this!" Rava said to him, "[Yes it can:] You have the fear of the king upon you, whereas we [in the World to Come] will not have the fear of the king upon us." [The gentile] answered, "Me? Why should I fear the king?" As they sat, an officer of the king approached and said to [the gentile], "Get up! The king has summoned you!" As [the gentile] emerged [from his bath], he said, "May the eyes of all those who await to see the downfall of your people be gouged out!" to which Rava answered, "Amen!" At that exact moment, [the gentile's] eye was gouged out.[3] Rava answered that the World to Come is inherently superior to this world, and that its pleasures are of a sublime nature which cannot be perceived through human senses. For the joy to be experienced in the World to Come exceeds by far the most intense physical pleasure that the human body is able to feel in this world. This is the reason the World to Come is not mentioned in Scripture even once. As the Sages say, "All the prophets only prophesied about the days of *Mashiach*, but regarding the World to Come it is written,[4] 'O God, no eye has seen it but You.' "[5] Rava proved that even if a person were to rule over the

---

1. *Tamid* 31a.
2. *Pirkei D'Rabbi Eliezer* Chapter 11.
3. *Avodah Zarah* 65a.
4. *Isaiah* 64:3.
5. *Berachos* 34b.

entire planet, one could still say about him, "all his days are painful, and his business is a vexation; even at night his mind has no rest. . ."[1] for as the Sages say, "The more possessions, the more worry."[2] This concept has been elaborated upon in various ethical works. For example, *Chovos Halevavos* warns against relying upon one's wealth or upon one's sons and daughters; if one does, one is likely to lose everything.[3] As the Sages say, "No one leaves this world with even half of his desires fulfilled,"[4] since the more one has, the more one desires. In contrast, the *neshamah* in the World to Come is secure in the knowledge that its portion is eternal, and that it will never be taken away from it. It is ensconced in an ambience of serenity where it once and for all finds true peace and happiness. As the Sages say, "In the World to Come there is no eating or drinking, procreation, business or trade, jealousy, hatred, or competition. Rather, the righteous sit with their crowns upon their heads and delight in the radiance of the Divine Presence."[5] For this reason the Talmud uses the term "his soul rests" in reference to the death of the righteous.[6] It is also the reason the Sages say, "Better is one hour of spiritual bliss in the World to Come than the entire life of this world."[7] We now understand the deeper intention of the wise men of the Negev, who answered Alexander's question so eloquently by saying, "All those who embark on a sea voyage do not feel at ease until they have reached dry land." With these words, they conveyed the message that as long as the *neshamah* is afloat on the tempestuous "sea" that is this world, it cannot experience true serenity — and hence, absolute pleasure — until it comes upon its portion in the World to Come — "dry land." Clearly, then, the greatest worldly pleasure cannot even begin to be compared to the spiritual ecstasy of eternal, complete and utter joy which awaits the *neshamah* in the World to Come.

וַיְהִי סַעַר גָּדוֹל בַּיָּם — there was such a mighty tempest in the sea

The sea represents this world,[8] and the mighty tempest represents the

---

1. *Ecclesiastes* 2:23.
2. *Pirkei Avos* 2:8.
3. *Chovos Halevavos Sha'ar Revi'i, Sha'ar Habitachon,* chapter 1.
4. *Koheles Rabbah* 1:34.
5. *Berachos* 17a.
6. Some mentions of this term are *Berachos* 42b, *Kesubos* 104a, and *Bava Metzia* 86a.
7. *Avos* 4:22.
8. *Vilna Gaon's* commentary on verse 1:3, s.v. וימצא אניה, "and found a ship."

ספר יונה / 24

Angel of Death,[1] which comes to take the *neshamah* of sinners who have been condemned by the heavenly tribunal. Note that in the Hebrew the term "mighty tempest" appears in the masculine even though it usually appears in the feminine (סְעָרָה גְדוֹלָה). Why has its gender been changed? The feminine form would also fit better with the first clause of the verse — "a mighty wind" — which carries the feminine gender. What is the significance of this change? In order to understand, we must first become more familiar with the process by which the forces of impurity take hold of a man's *neshamah*: First, the Evil Inclination entices man's physical body with worldly desires and induces it to commit transgressions. King Solomon called this stage of destruction "a sickening evil."[2] The *Zohar* elaborates: "Why is it called 'a *sickening* [evil]'? Because when [this evil spirit] resides upon human beings, it causes them to become miserly with their money. Delegates of charity funds approach, and the [evil spirit] protests and says to the individual, 'Do not give [them] your money!'; the poor come [for alms], and the [evil spirit] protests; the individual desires to spend money for his own needs, and [the evil spirit] protests. . . From the day it possesses a person, it is as grave a disease as terminal illness, which likewise prevents the person from either eating or drinking."[3] As mentioned earlier, the aspect of evil which brings man to sin is called "a mighty wind." We have also mentioned above that conceptually, man's body is feminine in relation to the *neshamah* (see 1:3, s.v. בָּאָה "bound for"). This explains why the term "a mighty wind" carries the feminine gender: Since this aspect of the Evil Inclination attacks man's physical body — which is feminine in relation to the *neshamah* — the verse appropriately uses the feminine gender. After the Evil Inclination succeeds in bringing a person to sin, it stands before the heavenly tribunal and demands that his *neshamah* now receive the full measure of punishment that it deserves for having committed that transgression. The Evil Inclination does not rest until the person is found guilty and a death sentence is issued against his *neshamah*. Then, it — the very same impure force that originally enticed the person to sin in the first place — is sent to the world and charged with taking the sinner's *neshamah*. The verse calls this second stage of the Evil Inclination's onslaught — the slaying of the

---

1. Commentary on verse 1:4, s.v. הטיל רוח גדולה, "cast a mighty wind."
2. *Ecclesiastes* 5:12.
3. *Zohar* Volume II, 65a.

sinner's *neshamah* — "a mighty tempest." We can therefore understand why the term is phrased in the masculine gender: Since the primary victim of the Evil Inclination is the sinner's *neshamah* — which is masculine in relation to the body — the verse appropriately uses the masculine gender. We see, then, that the impure force which entices a person to sin is *the very same force* that ultimately punishes that person for his sins and takes his *neshamah*. With this explanation, it is also possible to gain a deeper understanding of the Sages' statement that the "tempest" specifically selected Jonah's ship as its target, while other ships in the vicinity sailed by on perfectly calm waters.[1] The angels of destruction, which are represented by the mighty tempest, choose their victims in a very selective manner — they are only permitted to torment individuals who have sinned.

וְהָאֳנִיָּה חִשְּׁבָה לְהִשָּׁבֵר — that the ship threatened to be broken up.

As mentioned earlier, the ship represents man's physical body. Expounding on this analogy, the *Zohar* states, "Man then goes about in this world like a ship about to break in the ocean, as in the verse, 'Then HASHEM cast a mighty wind . . . that the ship threatened to be broken up' (*Jonah* 1:4). While in this world man sins, for he believes that he has escaped his Master, and that He does not oversee this world. "At this time, the Holy One, Blessed is He, casts 'a mighty wind.' It is the decree, which continually stands in the presence of the Holy One, Blessed is He, and demands in His presence that justice be executed against the person — this is [the wind] that came upon the ship."[2] When all is well, man's corporeal self believes it will live forever,[3] and that therefore it is completely free to immerse itself in worldly pleasures. However, the moment the individual receives the full measure of the punishment that he has incurred through his sins, his corporeal self suddenly falters. In the throes of severe illness, tormented by physical anguish, the person's corporeal self comes to a terrifying realization — it is actually going to die! The *neshamah* is also frightened by the prospect of death, since it knows that it will have to undergo a period of excruciating pain in

1. *Pirkei D'Rabbi Eliezer*, Chapter 10.
2. *Zohar* Volume II, 1990.
3. See *Zohar* Volume III, 126a.

purgatory as a consequence of the individual's sins. However, its fear is of a lesser degree than the body's, for the *neshamah* knows that it will not cease to exist forever — it will be given another opportunity to rectify itself through reincarnation, as it is written, "God does all these things with man two or three times."[1] In reference to this verse, the *Zohar* states: "The [souls] of sinners fly in the air until they attain absolvement for their sins, and then they enter the body a second time in order to purify it. If [the soul] behaves in a righteous manner, it will not be required to enter [the body] again; but if it does not [behave in a righteous manner], then [it will be required to enter the body] a third time, as it is written, 'God does all these things with man two or three times.' And if, heaven forbid, it does not act righteously all three times, it has no further means by which to rectify itself — this is the intention of the verse, 'it will surely be cut off.'[2] Therefore, human beings must be careful with their souls, for it may well be its last turn."[3] In contrast, the body knows that its death is irreversible, final and eternal. It is likened to an earthen vessel: When rendered impure, it may only be purified by shattering it;[4] and once shattered, it can no longer be repaired.[5] This explanation also clarifies the unusual wording of the verse — translated literally, the term וְהָאֳנִיָּה חִשְּׁבָה לְהִשָּׁבֵר means "and the ship *thought* it would be broken up." Most commentators take the personification of the ship figuratively, as reflected in our translation of the verse. Others interpret the expression to mean that *the sailors* "thought the ship would break up."[6] According to our understanding, however, the choice of words is precise: The ship represents the body, and the storm represents the punishment that ultimately puts an end to the body's existence. Hence, the "ship thought it would be broken up" is a very accurate description of the sinner's frame of mind as he lies on his deathbed.

---

1. *Job* 33:29.
2. *Numbers* 15:31.
3. *Midrash Hane'elam, Parashas Ki Teitzei*, s.v. מת בלא בנים.
4. *Leviticus* 6:21.
5. See *Sanhedrin* 52b.
6. See *Ibn Ezra*.

א/ה ה וַיִּירְאוּ הַמַּלָּחִים וַיִּזְעֲקוּ אִישׁ אֶל־אֱלֹהָיו וַיָּטִלוּ
אֶת־הַכֵּלִים אֲשֶׁר בָּאֳנִיָּה אֶל־הַיָּם לְהָקֵל
מֵעֲלֵיהֶם וְיוֹנָה יָרַד אֶל־יַרְכְּתֵי הַסְּפִינָה וַיִּשְׁכַּב

---

5. הַמַּלָּחִים — The sailors

On a deeper level, "the sailors" represent the faculties that guide the body — the brain, the heart and various other forces.

וַיִּזְעֲקוּ אִישׁ אֶל אֱלֹהָיו — and cried out, each to his own god;

When the Angel of Death is about to take someone's life, the individual's corporeal faculties scream out for help to the things he most treasured and worshipped throughout his lifetime — gold, silver and the pleasures of the flesh. These worldly endeavors are called "gods of silver and gods of gold."[1]

In reference to man placing his trust in such transient elements on the day of his death, the verse states, "*On that day* (i.e., on the day of their death) man will throw away his false gods of silver and his false gods of gold, which they made for him to prostrate himself . . ."[2] Similarly, it is written, "Their silver and gold will be unable to rescue them *on the day of God's fury;* . . . they will not fill their stomachs."[3] Likewise, "Wealth will not avail *in the day of wrath...*"[4] and "Those who rely on their possessions and are boastful of their great wealth...will leave their possessions to others."[5]

וַיָּטִלוּ אֶת הַכֵּלִים אֲשֶׁר בָּאֳנִיָּה אֶל הַיָּם — they cast the ship's wares overboard

The sailors on Jonah's ship threw all the cargo overboard. Similarly, as the disease brought on by the Angel of Death intensifies, the sinner removes his garments and collapses into bed.

לְהָקֵל מֵעֲלֵיהֶם — to lighten their load.

The simplest explanation of this verse is that the illness so weakens the sinner that even his garments begin to feel heavy to him, and he is forced to remove them. How ironic! Not only is he forced to leave behind

---

1. *Exodus* 20:20. See *Maggid Meisharim, Parashas Beshalach* and *Parashas Yisro* .
2. *Isaiah* 2:20.
3. *Ezekiel* 7:19.
4. *Proverbs* 11:4.
5. *Psalms* 49:7-11.

sailors became frightened and cried out, each to his own god; they cast the ship's wares overboard to lighten their load. But Jonah had descended to the boat's holds and had lain down

his beloved gold and silver upon his death, he is even forced to leave behind the very clothes he wears on his back. Alternatively, the verse teaches that if the sinner would give away his clothes to charity, he would significantly mitigate the severity of the evil decree issued against him (i.e., "lighten his load"). For as it is written, "Charity rescues from death."[1]

וְיוֹנָה יָרַד אֶל יַרְכְּתֵי הַסְּפִינָה — **But Jonah had descended to the boat's holds**

As mentioned above, Jonah represents the *neshamah*. His descent to the boat's holds is a metaphor for the *neshamah's* descent to the feet. This phenomenon occurs in the wake of sin, as explained in *Tikunei Zohar*: "Come and see: Some people move their eyes while they talk, others gesticulate with their hands, others move their head, others sway their body and others move their legs. The location of the *neshamah* is responsible for this — in whichever limb [the *neshamah*] is located, that is the limb that moves the most. R' Elazar said to him, 'But Father, isn't the *neshamah* located in a certain place in the heart, from where it spreads to all the other sections of the heart?' He answered him, 'My son, it has been written in reference to [the *neshamah*], "and she uncovered (וַתְּגַל, which can also mean "and she was exiled to") his feet and lay down"[2] — in accordance with the [evil] deeds of the person, [the *neshamah*] leaves its place and descends. The same is true of the Divine Presence, as it is written, "Your Mother (i.e., the Divine Presence) was sent away as a consequence of your transgressions."'[3] Complete repentance requires that one return [the *neshamah*] to its original place. . . In accordance with the individual's sins, it descends from one level to the next and from limb to limb until it eventually reaches the feet. Conversely, in accordance with the individual's merits, it gradually ascends until it reaches its original location."[4] In reference to this idea *Tikunei*

1. *Proverbs* 10:2.
2. *Ruth* 3:7.
3. *Isaiah* 50:1.
4. *Tikunei Zohar* 132b.

וַיֵּרָדַם: וַיִּקְרַב אֵלָיו רַב הַחֹבֵל וַיֹּאמֶר
לוֹ מַה־לְּךָ נִרְדָּם קוּם קְרָא אֶל־אֱלֹהֶיךָ
אוּלַי יִתְעַשֵּׁת הָאֱלֹהִים לָנוּ וְלֹא נֹאבֵד:

Zohar states, "Woe to the man whose *neshamah* descends down to his feet!"[1] The dust that surrounds the feet is, in the spiritual sense, the domain of the most concentrated evil and impure forces — it is the realm of the primordial serpent that caused Adam and Eve to sin.[2] Our verse teaches that by the time "the ship threatens to be broken up" — i.e., by the time a sinner's life is about to be taken by the Angel of Death as punishment for his sins — his *neshamah* (represented by Jonah) has surely descended to the harshest possible environment: down to the feet, the realm of the worst form of impurity.

Note the change in terminology that has taken place. Until this point in the narrative, the word אֳנִיָּה was used in reference to Jonah's ship. Now suddenly the word סְפִינָה appears. What is the significance of these two terms? The answer is that the term אֳנִיָּה suggests a large sea-faring vessel capable of sailing in the midst of the ocean, as is evident from the verse, "The way of the eagle in the heavens, the way of the snake upon the rock, *the way of the ship* (אֳנִיָּה) *in the heart of the high sea*. . ."[3] This mighty vessel that is capable of plying the high seas represents the body at the peak of its health, for as mentioned above, the sea represents this world and the shore represents the World to Come. A person who is strong and healthy becomes completely absorbed with matters of this world, while thoughts of "the shore" — the World to Come — are given secondary importance. However, as the body's strength wanes and the idea of death becomes more of a reality, "the shore" suddenly appears on the horizon. At this point, the once mighty sea-faring ship (אֳנִיָּה) is transformed into a frail boat (סְפִינָה) that finds itself hugging the coast. Since our verse portrays the moment of death, it fittingly refers to the ailing body as a boat (סְפִינָה). As for the previous verse, which discusses man in his prime, it fittingly speaks in terms of a ship (אֳנִיָּה).

וַיִּשְׁכַּב וַיֵּרָדַם — and he had lain down and fallen fast asleep

At the moment of death, a deep sleep overtakes the person's

---

1. *Tikunei Zohar* 50a.
2. *Vilna Gaon* on *Tikunei Zohar* 60b.
3. *Proverbs* 30:19.

and fallen fast asleep.

⁶ The ship's master approached him, and said to him, "How can you sleep so soundly? Arise! Call to your God. Perhaps God will pay us mind and we will not perish."

---

neshamah. This is the inner meaning of the verse, "And it happened, as the sun was about to set, a deep sleep fell upon Abram; and behold — a dread! a great darkness fell upon him"[1] — it alludes to the setting of the light of the *neshamah*, for Abraham, like Jonah, represents the *neshamah*.[2] In reference to this verse the *Zohar* states, "This is the day of harsh judgment that causes man to leave this world. For it has been taught: The time comes for man to leave this world. It is the day of awesome judgment, when the sun is eclipsed by the moon."[3]

6. וַיִּקְרַב אֵלָיו רַב הַחֹבֵל — The ship's master approached him,

The ship's master represents the dominant faculty that guides the body — the heart. As the *Zohar* explains, "When the Holy One, Blessed is He, created man in the world, he made him in the image of On High, and He placed his vitality and strength in the middle of his body — it is the place where the heart resides. [The heart] is the strength and source of sustenance of the entire body."[4]

וַיֹּאמֶר לוֹ מַה לְּךָ נִרְדָּם — and said to him, "How can you sleep so soundly?"

The *Zohar* teaches that the "master" of the body — the Good Inclination — rouses the *neshamah* from its deep sleep and pleads, "This is no time to sleep! You are being taken up to be judged for all you have done in this world. Repent for your sins!"[5]

קוּם קְרָא אֶל אֱלֹהֶיךָ — Arise! Call to your God.

The heart urges the soul to repent because the *neshamah's* roots emanate from On High.

אוּלַי יִתְעַשֵּׁת הָאֱלֹהִים לָנוּ וְלֹא נֹאבֵד — Perhaps God will pay us mind and we will not perish.

The heart beseeches the *neshamah* to repent in the hope that the evil

---

1. *Genesis* 15:12.
2. *Midrash Hane'elam, Parashas Lech Lecha,* s.v. שכרך הרבה מאד.
3. *Zohar* Volume I, 227a.
4. *Zohar* Volume III, 161b.
5. *Zohar* Volume II, 199.

זַ וַיֹּאמְרוּ אִישׁ אֶל־רֵעֵהוּ לְכוּ וְנַפִּילָה
גוֹרָלוֹת וְנֵדְעָה בְּשֶׁלְּמִי הָרָעָה הַזֹּאת לָנוּ
וַיַּפִּלוּ גּוֹרָלוֹת וַיִּפֹּל הַגּוֹרָל עַל־יוֹנָה:

---

decree will be rescinded. The urgent tone of the heart's plea stems from the knowledge that it, along with the rest of the body, will not be given another opportunity to achieve rectification. Once dead, they will not rise again. Not only the physical limbs of the body face eternal death. The same fate awaits the lower components of man's spiritual being — the bestial aspects of his *nefesh* and *ruach*. In very general terms, *nefesh* refers to the faculty that guides a person's actions, while *ruach* refers to the faculty that guides his speech.[1] These aspects of the person's being face eternal extinction as well, as it is written, "like his own dung, he will perish forever."[2] The *neshamah*, on the other hand, feels less anxiety. It knows that it will be reincarnated and given another chance to rectify itself.

7. וַיֹּאמְרוּ אִישׁ אֶל רֵעֵהוּ לְכוּ וְנַפִּילָה גוֹרָלוֹת וְנֵדְעָה בְּשֶׁלְּמִי הָרָעָה הַזֹּאת לָנוּ — **Then they said to one another, "Come, let us cast lots that we may determine on whose account this calamity is upon us."**

When a person dies because of his sins, as death approaches, the body's faculties and limbs desperately try to determine which aspect of the individual's being has brought on "this calamity." Perhaps the tongue, by having committed a transgression related to speech? Or perhaps the reproductive organs, by having committed a carnal sin?

וַיַּפִּלוּ גוֹרָלוֹת — **So they cast lots**

In this manner, the body's limbs and faculties attempt to determine which aspect of the individual has brought on the ailment.

וַיִּפֹּל הַגּוֹרָל עַל יוֹנָה — **and the lot fell on Jonah**

In the end the *neshamah* is held responsible, for it possesses the ability to influence the body to either good or evil. If the *neshamah* chooses to walk in the righteous path, it can transform the body — which is inherently inclined towards evil — into a purely good entity. On

---

1. The concept is elaborated in *Nefesh Hachaim*, Section 1, Chapter 15.
2. *Job* 20:7.

⁷ Then they said to one another, "Come, let us cast lots that we may determine on whose account this calamity is upon us." So they cast lots and the lot fell on Jonah.

the other hand, if the *neshamah* chooses evil, it can encourage the body to pursue its negative desires.

The potential of the *neshamah* to guide the body towards good is alluded to in *Avos*:

"[R' Yochanan ben Zakkai] said to [his disciples]: 'Go out and discern the proper way to which a man should cling.'

"R' Eliezer says, 'A good eye.' R' Yehoshua says, 'A good friend'. . .R' Elazar says, 'A good heart.'

"[R' Yochanan ben Zakkai] said to them: 'I prefer the words of Elazar ben Arach (i.e., 'a good heart') to your words, for your words are included in his words.' "[1]

What did R' Elazar mean by "a good heart"? An explanation may be found in *Tikunei Zohar*, where it is written, "The heart is the place where the *neshamah* resides."[2] In other words, R' Yochanan ben Zakkai agreed with R' Elazar that the most decisive factor in a person's spiritual growth is ultimately whether his heart — i.e., his *neshamah* — is inherently good. This quality outweighs all others.

On the other hand, the *neshamah* also has the potential to guide the body towards evil. This is evident from the verse, "The lawless *man* is a *man* of iniquity."[3] Here, "man" refers to the *neshamah*, which is masculine in relation to the body (as explained above).[4] And the verse continues, "he goes forth with distortion of the mouth, he winks with his eyes, shuffles with his feet, points with his fingers"[5] — the continuation of the verse depicts the manner in which a wicked *neshamah* will use the body's mouth, eyes, feet and hands to carry out its evil designs.

---

1. *Avos* 2:13.
2. *Tikunei Zohar*, Tikun 21, 59b.
3. *Proverbs* 6:12.
4. See commentary on verse 1:3.
5. *Proverbs* 6:12-13.

ח וַיֹּאמְרוּ אֵלָיו הַגִּידָה־נָּא לָנוּ בַּאֲשֶׁר לְמִי־
הָרָעָה הַזֹּאת לָנוּ מַה־מְּלַאכְתְּךָ֙ וּמֵאַ֣יִן
תָּב֔וֹא מָ֣ה אַרְצֶ֔ךָ וְאֵֽי־מִזֶּ֥ה עַ֖ם אָֽתָּה׃

---

8. וַיֹּאמְרוּ אֵלָיו הַגִּידָה נָּא לָנוּ בַּאֲשֶׁר לְמִי הָרָעָה הַזֹּאת לָנוּ — They said to him, "Tell us, now: In regard of whom has this calamity befallen us?

After determining that the body's ailment has come about through the fault of the *neshamah,* the body's limbs and faculties fear that they too will be implicated in the sin, and then be punished accordingly. With great trepidation they ask the *neshamah* to disclose who else will be punished along with it — i.e., the limbs and faculties of the body which took part in the transgression. This is the deeper intention of the words, "Tell us, now: In regard to *whom* has this calamity befallen us?"

מַה מְּלַאכְתְּךָ — What is your trade?

The limbs and faculties of the body question the *neshamah* further. They now demand that it reveal the nature of its mission ("trade") in this world.

וּמֵאַיִן תָּבוֹא — And from where do you come?

The body now admonishes the *neshamah* for having transgressed. In essence it asks, "How could you have forgotten your place of origin? Don't you know that you have roots in the heavenly realms? How could you have devoted all your days to the pursuit of earthly desires, and neglected the mission which God assigned to you?"

The Sages make numerous references to the *neshamah's* heavenly roots. For example, "It is written, 'And HASHEM God formed the man of dust from the ground, and He blew into his nostrils *the soul of life*'[1] — this refers to the holy *neshamah,* which is carved from the Throne of Glory of the Most High King."[2]

In light of its exalted origins, it is absolutely inappropriate for the *neshamah* to pursue earthly desires. As the *Zohar* states, "How great is man's obligation to contemplate and scrutinize himself every single day, to examine his deeds and scrutinize all his affairs. Let him contemplate the idea that the Holy One, Blessed is He, created and granted him an exalted *neshamah* and made him superior to all other

---

1. *Genesis* 2:7.
2. *Midrash Hane'elam, Parashas Bereishis,* s.v. תוצא הארץ נפש חיה.

[8] *They said to him, "Tell us, now: In regard to whom has this calamity befallen us? What is your trade? And from where do you come? What is your land? And of what people are you?"*

---

creations for only one purpose — to enable him to ponder His Divine service and adhere to Him. But not in order to indulge in vain pursuits!"[1]

מָה אַרְצֶךּ — What is your land?

The body continues to admonish the *neshamah,* saying, "How did you forget the land from which you came to this world?" The *Zohar* explains what is meant by the *neshamah's* "land":

"The Holy One, Blessed is He, placed [man] in *the land* inside the Garden of Eden, which He created in a secret and concealed place on earth in the form and image of On High. As it is written,[2] 'HASHEM God took man and placed him in the Garden of Eden, to work it and to guard it.' "[3] Similarly, "The Holy One, Blessed is He, taught man Torah. . . This is the intention of the verse, 'HASHEM God took man and placed him in the Garden of Eden' — this is the Garden of Torah. 'To work it' — these are the Torah's positive commandments. 'To guard it' — these are the Torah's negative commandments."[4]

We see that the *neshamah* descends to this world from the pristine "land" called the Garden of Eden, where the *neshamah* resided in an ambience of Torah and *mitzvos*. "How, then," the body demands of the *neshamah,* "could you have forgotten your land? How could you have stooped so low and violated the laws of the Torah?"

וְאֵי מִזֶּה עַם אָתָּה — And of what people are you?

When it is discovered that the *neshamah* neglected to observe the directives which God commanded to the Jewish People, its origins are called into question. Its wicked behavior is suspected to indicate the presence of gentile roots, as it is written, "They mingled with the nations and learned their deeds."[5]

---

1. *Midrash Hane'elam, Parashas Bereishis,* s.v. גן בעדן.
2. *Genesis* 2:15.
3. *Zohar Chadash, Shir Hashirim*, s.v. האדם הראשון.
4. *Tikunei Zohar*, Tikun 45, 101a.
5. *Psalms* 106:35.

אָ/ט־י ט וַיֹּאמֶר אֲלֵיהֶם עִבְרִי אָנֹכִי וְאֶת־יהֹוָה אֱלֹהֵי
הַשָּׁמַיִם אֲנִי יָרֵא אֲשֶׁר־עָשָׂה אֶת־הַיָּם
י וְאֶת־הַיַּבָּשָׁה: וַיִּירְאוּ הָאֲנָשִׁים יִרְאָה
גְדוֹלָה וַיֹּאמְרוּ אֵלָיו מַה־זֹּאת עָשִׂיתָ כִּי־

Indeed, the ancestry of a number of Jews can be traced to the mixed multitude,[1] to Amalek and to other nations, as explained in the *Zohar*.[2]

The entire verse can be understood in terms of the following passage from the *Zohar*:[3]

"At the time when the Holy One, Blessed is He, sends the *neshamah* from its holy place, He blesses it... As it is written, 'HASHEM said to Abram' — [Abram] is the *neshamah*. What does God say to the *neshamah*? 'Go for yourself from your land, from your birthplace and from your father's house, to the land that I will show you.'"[4]

"Go from your land" corresponds to the question asked of the *neshamah* by the body's limbs, "What is your land?"

"And from your birthplace" corresponds to the question asked of the *neshamah* by the body's limbs, 'And from where do you come?'

"And from your father's house" corresponds to the question asked of the *neshamah* by the body's limbs, 'And of what people are you?'

"To the land that I will show you" corresponds to the question asked of the *neshamah* by the body's limbs, 'What is your trade?' for (when God) told Abram, 'Go to the land that *I* will *show you*," He meant that He would show him what to do."

9. וַיֹּאמֶר אֲלֵיהֶם עִבְרִי אָנֹכִי — He said to them, "I am a Hebrew,

According to the simple understanding of the verse, Jonah answers the sailors' inquiries by informing them that he is a Hebrew.

However, according to our deeper interpretation that Jonah is the *neshamah* and the sailors are the body, Jonah's answer must be understood differently. The explanation is as follows:

The Hebrew word for "a Hebrew" (עִבְרִי) derives from the word עֵבֶר, which means "from beyond," as in the verse, "your forefathers...always

---

1. See *Exodus* 12:38.
2. *Raya Mehemna, Parashas Naso* 122b.
3. *Midrash Hane'elam, Parashas Lech Lecha,* s.v. לך לך מארצך.
4. *Genesis* 12:1.

⁹ *He said to them, "I am a Hebrew, and HASHEM, the God of the Heavens, do I fear, Who made the sea and the dry land."*

¹⁰ *The men were seized with great fear and they asked him, "What is this that you have done?" For*

dwelled beyond (בְּעֵבֶר) the river."¹ In this sense, the *neshamah* answers the body's inquiries by informing it that its origins are "from beyond" the River of Fire² — in other words, that the *neshamah* emerges from the Upper Garden of Eden and the Throne of Glory.

The *Zohar* describes the layout of the heavenly realm that the *neshamah* must traverse on its voyage from this world back to its source.

"At the time when the *neshamah* leaves this world, it undergoes various forms of retribution before it reaches the place of its origin. All souls must cross the River of Fire...and bathe in it. Who can ascend there and cross [the River of Fire] without great trepidation? Only the souls of the righteous can cross it fearlessly."³

This is the deeper meaning of the words "I am a Hebrew (עִבְרִי)" — i.e., I, the *neshamah*, come from beyond the River of Fire.

וְאֶת ה' אֱלֹהֵי הַשָּׁמַיִם אֲנִי יָרֵא — and HASHEM, the God of the Heavens, do I fear

This is the *neshamah's* answer to the question, "What is your trade?" — the *neshamah's* "trade" is to fear God.

אֲשֶׁר עָשָׂה אֶת הַיָּם וְאֶת הַיַּבָּשָׁה — Who made the sea and the dry land."

As mentioned earlier the sea represents this world, while the land represents the Garden of Eden and the world to come. The *neshamah* responds to the body's question, "What is your land?" by essentially saying, "I navigate the sea that is this world in order to fulfill God's *mitzvos*, and thereby make preparations to reach my home on the shore — the dry land that is the World to Come."

10. וַיִּירְאוּ הָאֲנָשִׁים יִרְאָה גְדוֹלָה וַיֹּאמְרוּ אֵלָיו מַה זֹּאת עָשִׂיתָ — The men were seized with great fear and they asked him, "What is this that you have done?"

Upon hearing the *neshamah's* account of its exalted heavenly origins

1. *Joshua* 24:2.
2. See *Daniel* 7:10, *Chagigah* 13b.
3. *Zohar Volume* I, 201a.

יָדְעוּ הָאֲנָשִׁים כִּי־מִלִּפְנֵי יהוה הוּא בֹרֵחַ
כִּי הִגִּיד לָהֶם: וַיֹּאמְרוּ אֵלָיו מַה־נַּעֲשֶׂה
לָּךְ וְיִשְׁתֹּק הַיָּם מֵעָלֵינוּ כִּי הַיָּם הוֹלֵךְ
וְסֹעֵר: וַיֹּאמֶר אֲלֵיהֶם שָׂאוּנִי וַהֲטִילֻנִי
אֶל־הַיָּם וְיִשְׁתֹּק הַיָּם מֵעֲלֵיכֶם כִּי יוֹדֵעַ
אָנִי כִּי בְשֶׁלִּי הַסַּעַר הַגָּדוֹל הַזֶּה עֲלֵיכֶם:

יא

יב

---

and the momentous task that it was assigned to carry out in this world,
the body confronts it with the question, "What have you done? If you are
aware of your true nature, then why have you behaved so wickedly until
now?"

כִּי יָדְעוּ הָאֲנָשִׁים כִּי מִלִּפְנֵי ה׳ הוּא בֹרֵחַ כִּי הִגִּיד לָהֶם — **For the men knew
that it was from before HASHEM's presence that he was fleeing, for he
had so told them.**

The body's limbs tremble with fear upon hearing the *neshamah's*
account of its exalted origins and weighty mission, for they have an
intimate knowledge of the negative deeds that the *neshamah* committed
ever since the very first day it entered the body. Until this moment, the
limbs had not realized that the *neshamah's* behavior was sinful. They
now panic at the thought of the punishment that is bound to befall them
for having cooperated with the *neshamah* in its flight away from God.

In this sense the *neshamah* "tells" the body's limbs of its transgressions — like a glove on a hand, the body perceives the *neshamah's*
subtlest motions.

11. וַיֹּאמְרוּ אֵלָיו מַה נַּעֲשֶׂה לָּךְ וְיִשְׁתֹּק הַיָּם מֵעָלֵינוּ כִּי הַיָּם הוֹלֵךְ וְסֹעֵר — **They
said to him, "What must we do to you that the sea subside from upon
us? — for the sea grows stormier."**

As mentioned earlier, the stormy sea represents the forces of
judgment and retribution.

After establishing the *neshamah's* guilt, the limbs of the body ask the
neshamah whether anything can be done to revoke the death sentence
decreed against the individual. They underscore the urgency of the
matter by emphasizing that "the sea grows stormier" — i.e., the
individual's punishment is growing more severe by the moment, causing
his condition to deteriorate rapidly.

1/11-12 *the men knew that it was from before HASHEM's presence that he was fleeing, for he had so told them.*

¹¹ They said to him, "What must we do to you that the sea subside from upon us? — for the sea grows stormier."

¹² He said to them, "Lift me up and heave me into the sea and the sea will calm down for you, for I know that it is because of me that this mighty tempest is upon you."

‫12. וַיֹּאמֶר אֲלֵיהֶם שָׂאוּנִי וַהֲטִילֻנִי אֶל הַיָּם וְיִשְׁתֹּק הַיָּם מֵעֲלֵיכֶם כִּי יוֹדֵעַ אָנִי כִּי‬ ‫בְשֶׁלִּי הַסַּעַר הַגָּדוֹל הַזֶּה עֲלֵיכֶם‬ — He said to them, **"Lift me up and heave me into the sea and the sea will calm down for you, for I know that it is because of me that this mighty tempest is upon you."**

As it looks into the eye of death, the *neshamah* comes to terms with its fate and advises the body to cast it overboard — i.e., to let the *neshamah* go and to undergo death. The *neshamah* has no other means by which to bring an end to the body's anguish.

Here, the term "lift me up" is used in the same context as in the verse "in three days Pharaoh will *lift your head* from you."[1] This term conveys a deeper meaning than meets the eye:

It is known that at the moment of death, the *neshamah* exits the body by way of the throat.[2] We have also established earlier that a person's sins cause the *neshamah* to descend from the heart to the feet.[3] Therefore, in order for the *neshamah* to experience death, it must be *lifted* upwards from the feet to the throat.

The deeper meaning of Jonah's request of the sailors to "heave me into the sea" is as follows:

As mentioned earlier, the ship represents man's body. Hence, by casting the *neshamah* out of the body and into the turbulent sea — which represents the forces of retribution — the body's agony will come to an end, and it will finally be left to rest in peace. For as the *Zohar* explains, "[The Satan's] greatest desire is to capture man's

1. *Genesis* 40:19.
2. *Zohar* Volume I, 98a.
3. Verse 1:5, s.v. ‫ויונה ירד‬ , *Jonah had descended*.

יג וַיַּחְתְּרוּ הָאֲנָשִׁים לְהָשִׁיב אֶל־הַיַּבָּשָׁה וְלֹא
יד יָכֹלוּ כִּי הַיָּם הוֹלֵךְ וְסֹעֵר עֲלֵיהֶם: וַיִּקְרְאוּ
אֶל־יהוֹה וַיֹּאמְרוּ אָנָּה יהוה אַל־נָא נֹאבְדָה
בְּנֶפֶשׁ הָאִישׁ הַזֶּה וְאַל־תִּתֵּן עָלֵינוּ דָּם
נָקִיא כִּי־אַתָּה יהוה כַּאֲשֶׁר חָפַצְתָּ עָשִׂיתָ:

spirit"[1] — therefore, the Satan loses all interest in the body as soon as the *neshamah* departs.

Likewise, the *Zohar* states: "We have established that the [spiritual force responsible for executing the] verdict of guilt is not placated until that time when it is written, 'They lifted Jonah' (ibid., 1:15) — [until] they carry [the sinner] from his house to the cemetery... What is written next? 'And heaved him into the sea, and the sea stopped its raging' (ibid.) — meaning, when they place him in the grave, which is the place of judgment, then the verdict of guilt that was so enraged is placated."[2]

13. וַיַּחְתְּרוּ הָאֲנָשִׁים לְהָשִׁיב אֶל־הַיַּבָּשָׁה וְלֹא יָכֹלוּ כִּי הַיָּם הוֹלֵךְ וְסֹעֵר עֲלֵיהֶם — Nevertheless, the men rowed hard to return to the shore, but they could not, because the sea was growing stormier upon them.

The body's faculties initially reject the *neshamah's* advice to succumb to death. Instead, they muster their last reserves and make a brave effort to "return to the shore" — i.e., to return to the ways of the Torah and thereby reach the "shore" of the World to Come.

However, its efforts are in vain, for repentance does not help once the evil mandate has already been decreed. As the Sages say:

"One verse says, 'I [God] do not desire the death of the one who should die,'[3] yet a different verse says, 'For God desired to kill them.'[4] How can this apparent contradiction be resolved?

"[The answer is that] *before* the evil mandate has been decreed, '[God] does not desire the death of the [wicked],one who should die,' but *after* the evil mandate has been decreed, 'For God desired to kill them.' "[5]

---

1. *Zohar* Volume III, 172b.
2. *Zohar* Volume II, 199b.
3. *Ezekiel* 18:32.
4. *I Samuel* 2:25.
5. *Sifrei*, *Nasso* 42, cited in *Tosfos* on *Niddah* 70b, s.v. כאן בעושה תשובה.

1/13-14 ¹³ *Nevertheless, the men rowed hard to return to the shore, but they could not, because the sea was growing stormier upon them.*

¹⁴ *Then they called out to* HASHEM, *and said, "O, please,* HASHEM, *let us not now perish on account of this man's soul and do not reckon it to us as innocent blood, for You,* HASHEM, *as You wished, so have You done."*

---

14. וַיִּקְרְאוּ אֶל ה' וַיֹּאמְרוּ אָנָּה ה' אַל נָא נֹאבְדָה בְּנֶפֶשׁ הָאִישׁ הַזֶּה וְאַל תִּתֵּן עָלֵינוּ דָּם נָקִיא — **Then they called out to** HASHEM **and said, "O, please,** HASHEM, **let us not now perish on account of this man's soul and do not reckon it to us as innocent blood,**

The physical faculties beseech God not to slay the body as a consequence of the *neshamah's* transgressions. They also entreat Him not to hold them accountable for the individual's premature death, which has occurred as a direct result of the sins which the body's physical faculties enabled him to commit.

כִּי אַתָּה ה' כַּאֲשֶׁר חָפַצְתָּ עָשִׂיתָ — **for You,** HASHEM, **as You wished, so have you done.**

The body's faculties attempt to draw a clear distinction between themselves and the *neshamah* in order to acquit themselves of guilt. They argue that the death penalty is only appropriate for the *neshamah* — considering its great potential for spiritual achievements, it surely deserves to be punished for having squandered its time in this world in the pursuit of earthly desires.

In contrast, the body should not be held culpable, for God Himself deemed that it be created from coarse earthly matter, and therefore, that it be inherently fallible. The body's faculties argue that they never had a chance, for they were destined to sin from their very inception. Therefore they should not be held liable for having taken part in sin, since God's will dictated that their nature be dominated by animal tendencies. This is the true intent of the verse, "For You, HASHEM, as You wished, so have You done" — the body is not at fault, for God created it as He saw fit.

The Sages illustrate the body's argument with the following analogy:

"Two men committed an offense against the monarch of their country; one of the men was a villager, the other was of noble stock. The king

וַיִּשְׂאוּ אֶת־יוֹנָה וַיְטִלֻהוּ אֶל־הַיָּם וַיַּעֲמֹד
טז הַיָּם מִזַּעְפּוֹ: וַיִּירְאוּ הָאֲנָשִׁים יִרְאָה גְדוֹלָה
אֶת־יהוה וַיִּזְבְּחוּ־זֶבַח לַיהוה וַיִּדְּרוּ נְדָרִים:

placed both criminals on a high platform, [tried them], and saw that both men had committed the very same infraction.

"What did the king do? He acquitted the villager and convicted the man of noble descent.

"The king's courtiers said to him, 'But your Highness — both men committed the very same infraction, and yet you acquit the villager and convict the nobleman?'

"The king answered, 'I acquitted the villager because he is completely ignorant of how one must conduct himself in the presence of royalty. The nobleman, on the other hand, is in my proximity every single day, and he is very familiar with the codes of conduct.'

"Likewise, the body is the villager, as in the verse, 'And HASHEM God formed the man of dust *from the ground.*'[1] The neshamah is the nobleman, as in the continuation of the verse, '. . .and He blew into his nostrils *the soul of life.*' "[2]

15. וַיִּשְׂאוּ אֶת יוֹנָה וַיְטִלֻהוּ אֶל הַיָּם וַיַּעֲמֹד הַיָּם מִזַּעְפּוֹ — **And they lifted Jonah and heaved him into the sea, and the sea stopped its raging.**

As the Angel of Death comes nearer and draws its sword, "the individual's neshamah bids each of the body's limbs farewell, just as a person bids his friend farewell before departing elsewhere.

"At that point, [the neshamah] says, 'Woe to me for what I have done!' However, [regret] only helps when the cure of repentance is applied before this critical moment."[3]

The neshamah then leaves the body and plunges into the "sea" of judgment. At that very moment, the "sea stops its raging" and the body grows still.

16. וַיִּירְאוּ הָאֲנָשִׁים יִרְאָה גְדוֹלָה אֶת ה' — **Then the men feared HASHEM greatly**

"The men" is a reference to the limbs of the body, which depart after

---

1. *Genesis* 2:7.

2. *Midrash Tanchuma, Vayikra* 6.

3. *Zohar* Volume III, 126b.

1/15-16   [15] *And they lifted Jonah and heaved him into the sea, and the sea stopped its raging.* [16] *Then the men feared HASHEM greatly and they offered a sacrifice to HASHEM and took vows.*

---

the *neshamah's* departure from the body — they are petrified with fear as they await death to overtake them.

The *Zohar*[1] describes this terrifying moment:

"On that dreadful and awesome day when the time comes for a person to leave the world, the four corners of the universe go into a state of intense judgment. . . A proclamation goes out to the upper world and it is heard in two hundred and seventy universes. If the individual is righteous, all the universes go out to welcome him in a state of joy. But if he is not righteous — woe to that man and woe to his portion!. . .

"[A black rooster] begins calling out between the gates. . . At first it calls out, 'Behold, the day of HASHEM is coming; (a day) of cruelty, rage and burning anger, to make the land desolate; and He will annihilate its sinners from it.'[2] Then it calls out a second time, saying, 'He forms mountains, and creates winds; He recounts to a person what were his deeds.'[3]

"At that moment, the individual sits and [listens] as his deeds give testimony before him, and he admits to all [that is said].

"At the moment when his *neshamah* is about to be taken out, the rooster calls out, saying, 'Who would not fear You, O King of the nations?' "[4]

וַיִּזְבְּחוּ זֶבַח לַה' וַיִּדְּרוּ נְדָרִים — and they offered a sacrifice to HASHEM and took vows.

In reference to the moment when the individual hears the testimony against him and he admits his guilt, the Sages say:

"[The souls of the deceased] agree with the verdict decreed against them — they say before Him, 'Master of the universe, You have judged fittingly, You have acquitted fittingly, You have convicted fittingly! You have fittingly prepared *Gehinnom* for the wicked and *Gan Eden* for the righteous!"[5]

---

1. *Zohar* Volume I, 218b.
2. *Isaiah* 13:9.
3. *Amos* 4:13.
4. *Jeremiah* 10:7.
5. *Eruvin* 19a.

ב/א־ב א וַיְמַן יהוה דָּג גָּדוֹל לִבְלֹעַ אֶת־יוֹנָה וַיְהִי יוֹנָה
בִּמְעֵי הַדָּג שְׁלֹשָׁה יָמִים וּשְׁלֹשָׁה לֵילוֹת:
ב וַיִּתְפַּלֵּל יוֹנָה אֶל־יהוה אֱלֹהָיו מִמְּעֵי הַדָּגָה:

As the Sages say, "The ways of the Holy One, Blessed is He, are unlike the ways of flesh and blood. The ways of flesh and blood dictate that a person who has been sentenced to death by the king be gagged in order to prevent him from cursing the king. In contrast, the ways of the Holy One, Blessed is He, are such that a person who has been sentenced to death holds his silence, as it is written, 'To You, silence is praise. . .'[1] Not only this, but he even utters praise, as it is written '[To You, silence is] praise.' Not only this, but he even feels as though he has brought a sacrificial offering, as it is written, 'and vows will be paid to You.' "[2]

This is the deeper meaning of the words "and they (i.e., the limbs of the body) offered a sacrifice to God and took vows" — the body accepts its punishment with understanding and love.

2.

1. וַיְמַן ה׳ דָּג גָּדוֹל לִבְלֹעַ אֶת יוֹנָה — Then HASHEM designated a large fish to swallow Jonah

The fish that swallowed Jonah represents the grave and the netherworld, which in a figurative sense "swallow" the *neshamah*. All souls in the netherworld are ruled by an angel fittingly named Dumah,[3] which in Hebrew means "silence," as in the verse, "neither the dead can praise God nor any who descend into silence. . ." (*Psalms* 115:17).

In reference to the *neshamah's* descent to the netherworld the *Zohar* states:

"We have established that the verdict of guilt is not placated until that time when it is written, 'They lifted Jonah' — [i.e., until] they carry the individual from his house to the cemetery. . . What is written next? 'And they heaved him into the sea, and the sea stopped its raging' — meaning, that the enraged attribute of Judgment is only placated when the individual is buried in the grave, for this is the place of Judg-

---

1. *Psalms* 65:2.
2. *Eruvin* 19a.
3. *Rashi* on *Berachos* 18b, s.v. דלמא דומה. There he writes that Dumah is "the angel that has been appointed over the dead."

¹Then HASHEM designated a large fish to swallow Jonah and Jonah remained in the fish's belly three days and three nights.

² Jonah prayed to HASHEM, his God, from the fish's belly.

---

ment. The fish that swallowed [Jonah] *is* the grave."¹

וַיְהִי יוֹנָה בִּמְעֵי הַדָּג שְׁלֹשָׁה יָמִים וּשְׁלֹשָׁה לֵילוֹת — **and Jonah remained in the fish's belly three days and three nights.**

During the first three days after death the *neshamah* feels an overwhelming desire to re-enter the body; it consequently hovers over it at all times. At the conclusion of the three-day period, however, the *neshamah* sees the body's facial disfigurement and abandons it forever.

The Sages describe the condition of the body and *neshamah* during the first three days in the grave:

"During the first three days [in the grave], the *neshamah* hovers above the body and is under the illusion that it will re-enter it. When it notices the [body's] facial disfigurement, it abandons the body and leaves. Following the three first days, the stomach splits open in [the person's] face and says to him, 'Take back all that you stole and robbed which you have placed within me!'

"R' Chagi said in the name of R' Yoshiah: This lesson is derived from the verse,² 'I will. . .spray dung — the dung of your festive offerings — in your faces.' "³

2. וַיִּתְפַּלֵּל יוֹנָה אֶל ה׳ אֱלֹהָיו מִמְּעֵי הַדָּגָה — **Jonah prayed to HASHEM, his God, from the fish's belly.**

Just as Jonah prayed to God from the belly of the fish, so does the *neshamah* pray to God from the depths of the netherworld. As the Sages say:

"What is the meaning of the verse, 'Those who pass through the Valley of Wailing turn it into a fountain. . .'?⁴ 'Those who pass' refers to individuals who transgress God's will; 'the Valley' means that they make their *Gehinnom* deeper; 'of Wailing' means that they cry and shed tears

---

1. *Zohar* Volume II, 199.
2. *Malachi* 2:3.
3. *Talmud Yerushalmi, Mo'ed Katan, Perek 3, Halachah 5.*
4. *Psalms* 84:7.

ב/ג-ד ג וַיֹּאמֶר קָרָאתִי מִצָּרָה לִי אֶל־יהוה וַיַּעֲנֵנִי מִבֶּטֶן שְׁאוֹל שִׁוַּעְתִּי שָׁמַעְתָּ קוֹלִי: ד וַתַּשְׁלִיכֵנִי מְצוּלָה בִּלְבַב יַמִּים וְנָהָר יְסֹבְבֵנִי

---

like a fountain. . ."[1]

מִמְּעֵי הַדָּגָה — from the fish's belly.

In the previous verse the Hebrew word for "fish" appears in the male gender (דָּג), while in this verse it appears in the female gender (דָּגָה).

The Sages of the Midrash explain that Jonah was first swallowed by a male fish which later spat him out, and that then he was swallowed by a female fish pregnant with 365,000 eggs.[2]

The Midrash's unusual account of Jonah's odyssey may also be understood according to our deeper interpretation of the Book of *Jonah*:

The words of the Sages parallel the fate of the *neshamah*. As mentioned earlier, the *neshamah* first descends to the netherworld and is placed under the jurisdiction of the angel Dumah — he is the "male fish." Later, the angel Dumah sends the *neshamah* to *Gehinnom*, which the Sages call "the female mate of the Side of Impurity"[3] — it is represented by the pregnant female fish, while its 365,000 eggs represent the 365,000 demons that are contained within this "female mate of the Side of Impurity."[4]

Hence, the previous verse refers to the descent of the *neshamah* to the domain of Dumah, which is masculine in relation to *Gehinnom* — accordingly, the male gender is used. In contrast, this verse refers to the *neshamah's* transfer from the netherworld to *Gehinnom*, which is "the *female* mate of the Side of Impurity" —accordingly, the female gender is used.

3. וַיֹּאמֶר קָרָאתִי מִצָּרָה לִי אֶל ה' וַיַּעֲנֵנִי מִבֶּטֶן שְׁאוֹל שִׁוַּעְתִּי שָׁמַעְתָּ קוֹלִי — He said, "I called, in my distress, to HASHEM and He answered me; from the belly of the netherworld I cried out — You heard my voice.

---

1. *Eruvin* 19a.

2. *Pirkei D'Rebbi Eliezer*, cited by *Rashi* on *Jonah*.

3. *Zohar* Volume III, 234b.

4. *Mishnas Chareidim*, *Maseches Makom Hakelipos* 1:2, based on *Eitz Chaim* 49:5.

2/3-4 ³ *He said, "I called, in my distress, to HASHEM, and He answered me; from the belly of the netherworld I cried out — You heard my voice. ⁴ You cast me into the depth, in the heart of the seas, the river whirled around me,*

Just as Jonah calls out to God from the belly of the fish, so too, the *neshamah* calls out to God from the depths of *Gehinnom*, saying, "Whenever I faced adversity during my lifetime, I would call out to You, and You would always answer me. Now I call out to You from the 'belly of the netherworld,' and I beseech You to answer me once more."

4. וַתַּשְׁלִיכֵנִי מְצוּלָה בִּלְבַב יַמִּים — You cast me into the depth, in the heart of the seas,

Just as Jonah is cast into the sea, so too, the *neshamah* is cast into the depth of darkness, where it is judged for its transgressions and purified of sin. As it is written, "He will vanquish our iniquities and cast all our sins into the *depths of the sea*"[1] — "the depths of the sea" refers to the lowest and darkest levels of *Gehinnom*.

וְנָהָר יְסֹבְבֵנִי — the river whirled around me,

The verse alludes to the River of Fire, about which the *Zohar* states:

"At the time when the *neshamah* leaves this world, it undergoes various forms of punishment. . . All *neshamos* must cross the River of Fire. . .and bathe in it."[2]

This is the deeper meaning of the verse, "and a river is poured on their foundations"[3] — meaning, that the River of Fire is poured upon the *neshamos* of the wicked in order to purge them of sin.

The Sages said in reference to this concept,

"The verse states, 'A river of fire streamed forth before Him; thousands upon thousands served Him; myriads upon myriads stood before Him. . .'[4]

"Upon what does [this river] pour down?

"R' Zutra son of Tuvia said in the name of Rav: 'It pours down upon the

---

1. *Micah* 7:19.
2. *Zohar* Volume I, 201a.
3. *Job* 22:16.
4. *Daniel* 7:10.

ה כָּל־מִשְׁבָּרֶיךָ וְגַלֶּיךָ עָלַי עָבָרוּ: וַאֲנִי אָמַרְתִּי נִגְרַשְׁתִּי מִנֶּגֶד עֵינֶיךָ אַךְ אוֹסִיף ו לְהַבִּיט אֶל־הֵיכַל קָדְשֶׁךָ: אֲפָפוּנִי מַיִם עַד־נֶפֶשׁ תְּהוֹם יְסֹבְבֵנִי סוּף חָבוּשׁ לְרֹאשִׁי:

---

heads of the wicked in *Gehinnom*, as the verse states,[1] 'God's storm has gone forth in fury; a whirlwind whirls and descends *upon the heads of the wicked*.' "[2]

Similarly, the Sages said, "Whoever speaks defamatory words [causes] God to say to the angel of *Gehinnom*, 'I shall judge him from above [by pouring fire upon him], and you judge him from below.' "[3]

כָּל מִשְׁבָּרֶיךָ וְגַלֶּיךָ עָלַי עָבָרוּ — **all of Your breakers and waves swept over me.**

After the *neshamah* has endured the punishment that it incurred by way of its sins, it cries out to God, "I have suffered enough! I have received my full measure of punishment, and the forces of retribution have unleashed all of their wrath upon me."

5. וַאֲנִי אָמַרְתִּי נִגְרַשְׁתִּי מִנֶּגֶד עֵינֶיךָ — Then I thought, "I was driven from Your sight,"

The *neshamah* had feared that it had been "driven from God's sight." This term refers to a state of eternal limbo where on the one hand the *neshamah* is barred from the World to Come, and on the other, is prevented from standing in judgment before the Holy Tribunal and being granted a second chance to live.

This suspended state is one of the three possible situations in which the *neshamah* of man may find itself if it is not permitted to enter *Gan Eden*. The two other possibilities are: to be reincarnated in inanimate state, or to be sent to *Gehinnom*.[4]

אַךְ אוֹסִיף לְהַבִּיט אֶל הֵיכַל קָדְשֶׁךָ — **but I will gaze again at Your Holy Sanctuary!**

The *neshamah* realizes that it has been placed in *Gehinnom* in order

---

1. *Jeremiah* 23:19.
2. *Chagigah* 13b.
3. *Erachin* 15b.
4. *Biurei HaGra* on *Agados Hashor, Berachos* 28b.

all of Your breakers and waves swept over me.
*⁵ Then I thought: 'I was driven from Your sight,' but
I will gaze again at Your Holy Sanctuary! ⁶ Waters
encompassed me to the soul, the Deep whirled
around me, reeds were tangled about my head.*

---

to be purged of sin so that it may enter the World to Come in a state of
absolute purity. This is the meaning of the verse "but I will gaze again at
Your Holy Sanctuary" — "Sanctuary" refers to the World to Come.

This stage of the *neshamah's* purification process in *Gehinnom* is
described in greater detail by the *Zohar*:

"Both [the body and the *neshamah*] are judged by the angel
Dumah. The body is judged in the grave until it turns to dust. The
neshamah undergoes a series of judgments by the fires of *Gehinnom* until it is decreed that it [has] received its punishment. After
it has received its punishment and. . .it becomes pure, the *neshamah*
ascends from *Gehinnom* and is purged of its sins in the same manner
as metal is smelted by fire. Angels then accompany it in its ascent
until it enters the lower *Gan Eden*, where it bathes in water and
spices. . ."[1]

6. אֲפָפוּנִי מַיִם עַד נֶפֶשׁ — Waters encompassed me, to the soul,

As it is written, "I sink into the deep thick mud and find no foothold;
I have come into the watery depths, the flood sweeps me away"[2] — the
Sages explain that "thick mud" is one of the seven names of *Gehin-
nom*.[3]

תְּהוֹם יְסֹבְבֵנִי — the Deep whirled around me,

The *neshamos* of the wicked are judged in the Deep — i.e., *Gehinnom*.

As the Sages say, "[The verse] describes the righteous in their
domicile and the wicked in their domicile. It describes the righteous in
their domicile, as it is written, 'I will feed them in good pasture, and they
will graze on the mountain heights of Israel. . .'[4] It describes the wicked

---

1. *Zohar* Volume III, 53a.

2. *Psalms* 69:3.

3. *Eruvin* 19a.

4. *Ezekiel* 34:14.

ב/ז-ט ז לְקִצְבֵי הָרִים יָרַדְתִּי הָאָרֶץ בְּרִחֶיהָ בַעֲדִי
לְעוֹלָם וַתַּעַל מִשַּׁחַת חַיַּי יהוה אֱלֹהָי:
ח בְּהִתְעַטֵּף עָלַי נַפְשִׁי אֶת־יהוה זָכָרְתִּי וַתָּבוֹא
ט אֵלֶיךָ תְּפִלָּתִי אֶל הֵיכַל קָדְשֶׁךָ: מְשַׁמְּרִים

---

in their domicile, as it is written,[1] 'God the Lord says, "I mourned on the
day when he went down to the pit; I covered him with *the Deep*..." ' "[2]

סוּף חָבוּשׁ לְרֹאשִׁי — reeds were tangled about my head

Here the word סוּף ("reeds") is also an allusion to the sword of the
Angel of Death, which puts an end (סוֹף) to the life of man.

The concept to be learned from the similarity between the wordסוֹף
and סוּף is that when a person commits a sin, a spirit of impurity from
the lowest spiritual level (סוֹף) grasps hold of him and enshrouds him in
the same manner as the reeds tangled about Jonah's head. As the Sages
said, "Whoever commits one transgression in this world, it grasps him
and walks before him on the Day of Judgment, as the verse says, 'They
are *grasped* in their course. . .'[3] Rabbi Elazar said: [The sin] is bound to
him like a dog, as the verse says, 'he would not listen to her to lie with
her, to be with her'[4] — 'to lie with her' in this world, and 'to be with her'
in the world to come."[5]

Similarly the verse says, "The sins of the wicked man shall trap him,
he will be *caught* in the ropes of his own transgressions" (*Proverbs* 5:22).
This teaches that when a person violates one of the *mitzvos*, he attracts
to himself a spirit of the lowest (סוֹף) form of impurity, as the Sages said,
"Whoever defiles himself from below, he is defiled from above."[6] This
impure spirit then clings to him with all its strength.

This is the deeper intention of the verse, "reeds (סוּף) *were tangled*
about my head."

The *neshamah* continues to descend to the lowest levels of *Gehinnom*
and undergoes further purification.

---

1. *Ezekiel* 31:15.
2. *Bereishis Rabbah* 33:1.
3. *Job* 6:18.
4. *Genesis* 39:10.
5. *Sotah* 3b.
6. *Yoma* 39a.

2/7-9   [7] *To the bases of the mountains did I sink; the earth — its bar against me forever. Lift my life up from the pit, HASHEM, my God.* [8] *While my soul was faint within me, I remembered HASHEM; my prayer came to You, to Your Holy Sanctuary.* [9] *Those who observe*

It feels as if it is destined to stay in *Gehinnom* forever, as it is written, "Whoever descends to the netherworld does not come up."[1]

At this point it desperately calls out to God, "Lift my life up from the pit!"

8. בְּהִתְעַטֵּף עָלַי נַפְשִׁי אֶת ה' זָכָרְתִּי וַתָּבוֹא אֵלֶיךָ תְּפִלָּתִי אֶל הֵיכַל קָדְשֶׁךָ —
While my soul was faint within me, I remembered HASHEM; my prayer came to You, to Your Holy Sanctuary.

The *neshamah* begins to recount how it turned to God in the midst of its illness and pleaded for mercy.[2] For even though repentance performed under such duress is certainly not the most desirable form of repentance, it is nevertheless written, "You return man until he is impaired, and You decree, 'Repent, you mortals!' "[3] — i.e., repentance is accepted even when the sinner is "impaired."[4]

Although this repentance cannot save the sinner from death once the "evil mandate" — i.e., the death sentence — has been decreed,[5] this belated repentance *does* help to raise the *neshamah* out of *Gehinnom* after it has been purged of its sins. In reference to this concept the *Zohar* states:

"We have learned that a person who descends to [the last level of *Gehinnom*] will never again emerge — he is annihilated and destroyed from all the universes. . .

"But is it not written, 'from the *belly of the netherworld* I cried out — *You heard my voice,*'[6] [which implies that the *neshamah does* ascend from the last level of *Gehinnom*]? Likewise it is written, 'HASHEM . . . casts down to the netherworld and *raises up*'!"[7]

---

1. *Job* 7:9.
2. See notes on verse 1:13.
3. *Psalms* 90:3.
4. *Ruth Rabbah* 6:4.
5. *Sifrei, Nasso* 42, cited in *Tosfos* on *Niddah* 70b, s.v. *kan be'osse teshuvah*.
6. *Jonah* 2:3.
7. *I Samuel* 2:6.

ב/י , הַבְלֵי־שָׁוְא חַסְדָּם יַעֲזֹבוּ: וַאֲנִי בְּקוֹל תּוֹדָה
אֶזְבְּחָה־לָּךְ אֲשֶׁר נָדַרְתִּי אֲשַׁלֵּמָה יְשׁוּעָתָה לַיהוָה:

"The difficulty may be resolved as follows: The latter two verses refer to a *neshamah* that repented for its sins, whereas we refer to a *neshamah* which did not repent for its sins."[1]

Furthermore, the *Zohar* states that even thinking of repentance a moment before death eventually saves the *neshama* in *Gehinnom*.[2]

9. מְשַׁמְּרִים הַבְלֵי שָׁוְא חַסְדָּם יַעֲזֹבוּ — Those who observe folly, they forsake their kindness.

The *neshamah* continues to list its merits by asserting that during its lifetime it did not behave as "those who observe folly" — i.e., those who hoard worldly possessions until their last breath.

Such people are the subject of ridicule in the verse, "Man walks in absolute darkness, craving after absolute emptiness, amassing without knowing who will gather in."[3] Similarly, the verse states, "Thus I hated all my achievements laboring under the sun, for I must leave it to the man who succeeds me. And who knows whether he will be wise or foolish? Yet he will have control of all my possessions for which I toiled. . . This too is futility."[4]

If the desire to amass wealth is considered "folly" when the person is in good health, how much more so when he lies prone on his deathbed!

This idea leads us to a more basic question: Since the pursuit of worldly riches is "folly," is there a redeeming quality to wealth? The answer is "Yes."

God grants wealth to people for only one purpose — that they may perform acts of lovingkindness. Wealth should therefore not be regarded as one's personal possession; rather, a person should relate to his money as though it were a charity fund, and he, its administrator. He must strive to adopt this attitude in every stage of his life, but especially when he feels that death is near.

The verse therefore teaches that those who spend their money exclusively for their own needs "forsake" its true purpose — to bestow "their kindess" onto others.

---

1. *Zohar* Volume III 285b-286a.
2. *Zohar, Parashas Terumah* 150b.
3. *Psalms* 39:7.
4. *Ecclesiastes* 2:18-19.

---

10. וַאֲנִי בְּקוֹל תּוֹדָה — But as for me, with a voice of gratitude

The Hebrew word תּוֹדָה (translated here as "gratitude") can also mean "to confess," as in the verse, "Ezra the priest rose and said to them, 'You have trespassed by bringing home foreign wives, thus aggravating the guilt of Israel. Now *confess* (תוֹדָה) to HASHEM, the God of your forefathers. . .' "[1]

This interpretation of the word is in consonance with the secondary meaning of the Book of *Jonah* — as mentioned earlier, after the *neshamah* undergoes purification in purgatory, it begins to confess its sins in the presence of God.

אֱזְבְּחָה לָּךְ — Will I bring offerings to You;

By confessing one's sins it is possible to erase the faults of the past and reestablish a close relationship with God. In reference to this the Sages said,

"Come and see how the attributes of God differ from the attributes of flesh and blood:

"When a person angers his fellow, it is doubtful whether he will succeed in appeasing him. And even if he will manage to appease him, it is doubtful whether he will manage to do so through words alone.

"Not so, the ways of God — even when a person commits a transgression in secrecy, he can appease Him with words, as the verse says, 'Take *words* with you and return to HASHEM.'[2] Not only [is God appeased,] but He even shows favor to the individual, as the verse continues, 'accept what is *good.*' Furthermore, the person is considered by Scripture as actually having brought a sacrificial offering, as the verse says, 'we offer confession in place of bullocks.'

"And lest you argue [that 'bullocks'] refers to bullocks of a sin-offering, Scripture teaches, 'I will heal them from their rebelliousness and I will love them *generously*'[3] [— as though they had *generously* offered a gift-offering]."[4]

---

1. *Ezra* 10:10-11.
2. *Hosea* 14:3.
3. *Hosea* 14:5.
4. *Yoma* 86b.

יא   וַיֹּאמֶר יהוה לַדָּג וַיָּקֵא אֶת־יוֹנָה אֶל־הַיַּבָּשָׁה:

א-ב   וַיְהִי דְבַר־יהוה אֶל־יוֹנָה שֵׁנִית לֵאמֹר: קוּם לֵךְ
אֶל־נִינְוֵה הָעִיר הַגְּדוֹלָה וּקְרָא אֵלֶיהָ אֶת־
ג   הַקְּרִיאָה אֲשֶׁר אָנֹכִי דֹּבֵר אֵלֶיךָ: וַיָּקָם יוֹנָה וַיֵּלֶךְ
אֶל־נִינְוֵה כִּדְבַר יהוה וְנִינְוֵה הָיְתָה עִיר־גְּדוֹלָה

---

11. הַיַּבָּשָׁה אֶל יוֹנָה אֶת וַיָּקֵא לַדָּג ה' וַיֹּאמֶר — Then HASHEM addressed
the fish and it spewed Jonah out to the dry land.

When the *neshamah's* purification process is complete, God commands the angel Dumah — which is represented by the fish — to return
the *neshamah* to Him.

The angel Dumah obeys and sends the *neshamah* to *Gan Eden*,
which, as mentioned earlier, is represented by "dry land."

3.

1. שֵׁנִית יוֹנָה אֶל ה' דְבַר וַיְהִי – And the word of HASHEM came to Jonah
a second time,

The *neshamah* is sent to this world a second time and given another
opportunity to rectify the negative effects of its sins. As the *Zohar* states,
"The wicked are punished until their sin is absolved; thereafter, they are
reincarnated."[1]

Similarly, *Zohar* states: "[It is written,] 'Behold, You have banished me
this day from the face of the earth — can I be hidden from Your
presence? I must become a vagrant and a wanderer on earth; whoever
meets me will kill me.'[2] This verse alludes to the reincarnation of the
wicked, regarding which it has been written, 'And then I saw the wicked
buried and newly come. . .'[3]

" 'Behold, You have banished me this day' refers to the *neshamah's*
first incarnation; 'I must become a vagrant' refers to its second incarnation; 'and a wanderer' refers to its third incarnation."[4]

2. דִּבֵּר אָנֹכִי אֲשֶׁר הַקְּרִיאָה אֶת אֵלֶיהָ וּקְרָא הַגְּדוֹלָה הָעִיר נִינְוֵה אֶל לֵךְ קוּם
אֵלֶיךָ — "Arise! Go to Nineveh the great city, and cry out to her the

---

1. *Zohar Chadash* 72b.
2. *Genesis* 4:14.
3. *Ecclesiastes* 8:10.
4. *Tikunei Zohar, Tikun* 69.

2/11   ¹¹ *Then H*ASHEM *addressed the fish and it spewed Jonah out to the dry land.*

3/1-3   ¹ **A**nd *the word of H*ASHEM *came to Jonah a second time, saying,* ² *"Arise! Go to Nineveh the great city, and cry out to her the proclamation which I tell you."*

³ *So Jonah rose up and went to Nineveh, in accordance with H*ASHEM*'s word; Nineveh was a large city*

---

proclamation which I tell you."

As mentioned earlier (see commentary on verse 1:2), God commands the *neshamah* to leave *Gan Eden* and descend to this world, which is represented by the city of Nineveh, a name derived from the Hebrew term *Naveihu*, נָוֵהוּ, "His abode." The *neshamah* is instructed to impart knowledge to "the inhabitants of the city" — i.e., to the limbs of the body — in order that they may successfully resist forbidden physical temptations and rectify their sin.

The same applies to the *neshamah's* second journey to this world — it is again entrusted with the very same mission that it failed to fulfill during its first journey. In this sense, the verse can be interpreted to mean, "Go to Nineveh. . .and cry out to her the proclamation which *I have told you*," for God assigns the *neshamah* the original mission which it failed to fulfill during its previous incarnation.

3. וַיָּקָם יוֹנָה וַיֵּלֶךְ אֶל נִינְוֵה כִּדְבַר ה׳ — So Jonah rose up and went to Nineveh, in accordance with HASHEM**'s word;**

Just as Jonah "rose up" and went to Nineveh "in accordance with God's word," so too, the *neshamah* "rises up" upon its second incarnation and descends to this world with the intention to fulfill its mission in accordance with God's word.

וְנִינְוֵה הָיְתָה עִיר גְּדוֹלָה — Nineveh was a large city

Earlier we explained that man is called a "small city," as in the verse, "There was *a small city* with only a few inhabitants. . .'¹ In reference to this verse the Sages said, " 'A small city' refers to the human body; 'a few inhabitants' refers to the limbs of the body."²

---

1. *Ecclesiastes* 9:14.
2. *Nedarim* 32b; *Koheles Rabbah* 9:22.

לֵאלֹהִים מַהֲלַךְ שְׁלֹשֶׁת יָמִים: וַיָּחֶל יוֹנָה ד
לָבוֹא בָעִיר מַהֲלַךְ יוֹם אֶחָד וַיִּקְרָא
וַיֹּאמַר עוֹד אַרְבָּעִים יוֹם וְנִינְוֵה נֶהְפָּכֶת:

Here, the verse draws a clear distinction by emphasizing that "Nineveh was a *large* city." In other words, it stresses that the name "Nineveh" does not represent man, the "small city," but rather the corporeal world at large, called the "great city."

לֵאלֹהִים מַהֲלַךְ שְׁלֹשֶׁת יָמִים — to God, a three days' journey.

It is man's obligation to walk in the ways of God all the days of his life. As the *Rema* states in the very first law in the *Shulchan Aruch*, "It is written, 'I have set HASHEM before me always'[1] — this is an essential principle in Torah, and in the steps of the righteous who walk before God."

Practically, however, the masses (represented by the city of Nineveh) recall this awesome obligation on only three annual occasions — *Rosh Chodesh Elul*, *Rosh Hashanah* and *Yom Kippur*.

On *Rosh Chodesh Elul* the *shofar* rouses people from their spiritual slumber, as it is written, "Is a *shofar* ever sounded in a city and the people not tremble?"[2] Eventually, though, even the *shofar's* powerful effect wanes. People grow accustomed to its sound and gradually settle back into their daily routine.

Precisely because of this human tendency, the *shofar* is not sounded on *Erev Rosh Hashanah*. This interruption is meant to resensitize people to the *shofar's* message — to repent for their sins and return to the ways of God.

The *shofar* is just one example of how powerful external stimuli can become ineffective when used over a prolonged period of time — in this case, just thirty days. The Talmud speaks of this phenomenon in the following anecdote:

"A storm caught [Titus the Wicked] on the high seas and threatened to drown him. He said, 'It seems to me that the God of [Israel] can only manifest His strength through water. . . If He is truly a warrior, let Him come to shore and wage war against me!'

"A heavenly voice proclaimed, 'Wicked man, son of a wicked man,

---

1. *Psalms* 16:8.
2. *Amos* 3:6.

to HASHEM, a three days' journey. ⁴ *Jonah com-*
menced to enter the city, a distance of one day's
journey, then he proclaimed and said, "Forty days
more and Nineveh shall be overturned!"

---

descendant of Esau the wicked! I have an insignificant creature in My
world called a mosquito. . . Come to shore and wage war against it!'

"[Titus] came to shore, and a mosquito entered his nostril and gnawed
at his brain for seven years. One day he passed by the entrance of a
blacksmith's shop. [The mosquito] heard the sound of hammering, and
it became still. At this, Titus exclaimed, 'This is the cure!'

"Thereafter, he came to the blacksmith's shop every day. . .*for thirty*
days. After [thirty days], [the mosquito] *grew accustomed [to the noise*
and continued eating away at Titus' brain]."[1]

In this respect, mankind is akin to the mosquito — it becomes obliv-
ious to exterior stimuli after being exposed to it thirty consecutive days.

Aware of this human tendency, we refrain from blowing the *shofar* on
the day prior to *Rosh Hashanah* in order to maximize its impact upon us
on *Rosh Hashanah*.

The names of these three yearly occasions when we remember our
obligation to walk in God's ways are alluded to in the verse, "A lion
(אַרְיֵה) has roared; who will not fear? The Lord HASHEM ELOHIM has spok-
en; speaks, who will not prophesy?"[2] The *aleph* (א) of "lion" represents
Elul (אֱלוּל), the *reish* (ר) represents *Rosh Hashanah* (רֹאשׁ הַשָּׁנָה), and the
yod (י) and *hei* (ה) represent *Yom HaKippurim* (יוֹם הַכִּפּוּרִים).

This is alluded to in the words "to God, a three days' journey" — the
world at large walks in God's ways only three times a year.

**4. וַיָּחֶל יוֹנָה לָבוֹא בָעִיר מַהֲלַךְ יוֹם אֶחָד — Jonah commenced to enter the
city, a distance of one day's journey,**

"One day's journey" alludes to the first of the three yearly occasions
when people recall their obligation to walk in God's ways — namely,
Rosh Chodesh Elul.

On this day, the *neshamah* rebukes man for his transgressions.

וַיֹּאמַר עוֹד אַרְבָּעִים יוֹם — and said, "Forty days more"

The *neshamah* bids man to repent for his sins on *Rosh Chodesh Elul.*

---

1. *Gittin* 56b.
2. *Amos* 3:8.

ה וַיַּאֲמִינוּ אַנְשֵׁי נִינְוֵה בֵּאלֹהִים וַיִּקְרְאוּ־צוֹם
ו וַיִּלְבְּשׁוּ שַׂקִּים מִגְּדוֹלָם וְעַד־קְטַנָּם: וַיִּגַּע
הַדָּבָר אֶל־מֶלֶךְ נִינְוֵה וַיָּקָם מִכִּסְאוֹ וַיַּעֲבֵר
אַדַּרְתּוֹ מֵעָלָיו וַיְכַס שַׂק וַיֵּשֶׁב עַל־

It reminds him that he still has plenty of time — forty days remain until
Yom Kippur.

וְנִינְוֵה נֶהְפָּכֶת — **and Nineveh shall be overturned!"**

The decree of those who fail to repent is sealed forty days later, on
Yom Kippur. As the Sages say, "Man is judged on *Rosh Hashanah* and his
decree is sealed on *Yom Kippur*."[1]

5. וַיַּאֲמִינוּ אַנְשֵׁי נִינְוֵה בֵּאלֹהִים וַיִּקְרְאוּ צוֹם — **And the people of Nineveh
believed in God, so they proclaimed a fast**

The verse alludes to the Ten Days of Repentance between *Rosh
Hashanah* and *Yom Kippur*, in reference to which the *Midrash* states:

"On *Erev Rosh Hashanah* the spiritual leaders of the generation fast,
and God forgives a third of [Israel's] sins. People of average piety fast
during the days between *Rosh Hashanah* and *Yom Kippur*, and God
forgives [an additional] third of [Israel's] sins. On *Yom Kippur* all of Israel
fast and ask for mercy — men, women and children — and God forgives
all [their remaining transgressions]."[2]

וַיִּלְבְּשׁוּ שַׂקִּים מִגְּדוֹלָם וְעַד קְטַנָּם — **they. . .donned sackcloth, from their
great to their small.**

In the days of old it was customary for people to don sackcloth during
public fasts.

For example, the verse states, "When Ahab heard these words, he tore
his clothes, and *placed sackcloth upon his skin, and fasted*."[3] Similarly, it
is written, "In every province, any place the king's command and his
decree extended, there was great mourning among the Jews, and *fasting*
and weeping and lament; *sackcloth* and ashes were spread out for the
masses."[4]

1. *Rosh Hashanah* 16a.
2. *Tur Orach Chaim* 581, quoting from *Midrash Tanchuma, Parashas Emor* 22.
3. *I Kings* 21:27.
4. *Esther* 4:3.

⁵ *And the people of Nineveh believed in God, so they proclaimed a fast and donned sackcloth, from their great to their small.*

⁶ *The matter reached the king of Nineveh, he rose from his throne and removed his robe from upon himself; he covered himself with sackcloth and sat on*

In reference to this custom the Sages said, "Why do we don sackcloth? R' Chiya son of Abba said: 'In order to attest that we are equivalent to animals,' "¹ which people saddle with sackcloth.²

6. וַיִּגַּע הַדָּבָר אֶל מֶלֶךְ נִינְוֵה — The matter reached the king of Nineveh.

The call to repentance is of greater consequence to the king than to his subjects, for as the Sages say, "When a king and the public [come before the court], the king enters first to be judged, as it is written 'That He may grant the just due of His servant (i.e., King Solomon) and the just due of His people Israel, each day's need in its day.'³ — the king [enters] first, and afterwards the people.

"What is the reason [the king enters first to be judged]?

"One possible answer is that it would be disrespectful to keep the king waiting outside [the Chamber of Judgment]. Alternatively, it is fitting to [let the king be judged] before [God's] wrath intensifies."⁴

וַיָּקָם מִכִּסְאוֹ וַיַּעֲבֵר אַדַּרְתּוֹ מֵעָלָיו — he rose from his throne and removed his robe from upon himself;

The king's robe represents all the trappings of royalty that instill arrogance in the hearts of rulers, and which in turn bring them to sin. The susceptibility of rulers to succumb to sin is discussed in the *Zohar*:

"The verse states, 'When a ruler sins, commits one from among all the commandments of HASHEM his God that may not be done — unintentionally — and becomes guilty.'⁵

"R' Yitzchak taught: What is the difference between [this verse, which begins '*When* a ruler. . .'] and all other occasions in Scripture, where the verse begins '*If*'? For example, it is written, '*If* the anointed Kohen will

1. *Taanis* 16a.
2. *Rashi,* loc. cit.
3. *I Kings* 8:59.
4. *Rosh Hashanah* 8b.
5. *Leviticus* 4:22.

sin. . .,'[1] and *'If the entire assembly of Israel shall err. . .'*[2] Here the verse states, *'When a ruler sins,'* and not *'If a ruler will sin.'* What does this teach us?

"[The answer is] that it is highly unlikely that a priest would sin, since he is constantly scrupulous in his deeds, for the burden of his Master is upon him daily. . . Therefore, it is written in reference to priests, *'If the anointed Kohen will sin. . .'* Similarly, it is highly unlikely the entire congregation of Israel would commit a particular sin. . . For this reason it is written, *'If the entire assembly of Israel shall err. . .'*

"In contrast, here the verse states, *'When a ruler sins. . .'* — in other words, he will *surely* sin, for the knowledge that the people are his subjects *fills his heart with pride. . .* For this reason the verse states, *'When a ruler sins'. . .*and not *'If,'* for there is no doubt that he will sin."[3]

When rulers are judged by God, however, they are stripped of their might and power and are judged solely on the basis of their deeds. This is the true intent of the verse, "He rose from his throne and removed his robe from upon himself."

This insight clarifies the following enigmatic teaching of the Sages:

"Why is the *shofar* blown [on *Rosh Hashanah*]. . .when [the congregation] is sitting, and is then blown again when [the congregation] is standing? In order to confuse the Satan."[4]

In reference to this statement, *Tosfos* write the following:

"As is stated in *Talmud Yerushalmi*. . ., 'When the Satan first hears the sound of the *shofar* [on *Rosh Hashanah*], he becomes somewhat anxious. But when he hears it the second time, he exclaims, 'That must be the sound of the *shofar* mentioned in the verse [which describes the arrival of the Messiah] — 'It shall be on that day that a great *shofar* will be blown, and those who are lost in the land of Assyria and those cast away in the land of Egypt will come [together], and they will prostrate themselves to God on the holy mountain in Jerusalem.'[5] My end is near!'

"The Satan then becomes disoriented and is rendered incapable of demanding that Israel be punished for its sins."

Even with *Tosfos'* explanation, however, it remains unclear why the Satan confuses the blowing of the *shofar* of *Rosh Hashanah* with the

---

1. *Leviticus* 4:3.
2. Ibid., 4:13.
3. *Zohar* Volume III, 23a.
4. *Rosh Hashanah* 16b.
5. *Isaiah* 27:13.

shofar blasts that will herald the arrival of the Messiah.

The answer is as follows:

The two soundings of the *shofar* on *Rosh Hashanah* are alluded to in the verse, "Make for yourself two silver trumpets. . . When they sound a long blast with [both of] them, *the entire assembly* shall convene to you. . . If they sound a long blast with one, *the leaders* shall convene to you, *the heads of Israel's thousands*"[1] — one trumpet convenes the leaders, and two trumpets convene the entire assembly.

Accordingly, the first blast of the *shofar* on *Rosh Hashanah* (represented by the *one* trumpet in the verse) calls Israel's leaders to judgment, for as mentioned earlier, "When a king and the public [come before the court], the king enters first to be judged."[2] The second blast of the *shofar* (represented by the *two* trumpets in the verse) calls the entire assembly to judgment.

Therefore, the Satan is not overly concerned when he hears the first sounding of the *shofar*, for he knows that it is only Israel's rulers who are being called to judgment. From past experience he has learned that they are unlikely to repent for their sins on the Day of Judgment, for just as their pride makes them vulnerable to sin, it also hinders their hearts from feeling sincere regret for their misdeeds. The Satan becomes somewhat blustered, but not seriously concerned.

The second sounding of the *shofar*, on the other hand, paralyzes the Satan with fright, for it calls the nation's masses to judgment. The Satan has no doubts that they will repent wholeheartedly for their sins, thereby hastening the advent of the Messiah and the eternal and utter destruction of all evil, including himself.

The concept of Israel's repentance bringing about the advent of the Messiah is conveyed in the following Talmudic anecdote:[3]

"R' Yehoshua ben Levi found Elijah the Prophet standing at the entrance to R' Shimon bar Yochai's cave. . .

" 'When is the Messiah coming?" he asked [Elijah].

"Elijah answered, 'Go and ask him'. . .

"[R' Yehoshua] went to [the Messiah] and said, 'Shalom to you, my teacher and master. . . When will you come?'

" 'Today' the Messiah answered.

---

1. *Numbers* 10:2-4.

2. *Rosh Hashanah* 8b.

3. *Sanhedrin* 98a.

הָאֵפֶר: וַיִּזְעַק וַיֹּאמֶר בְּנִינְוֵה מִטַּעַם הַמֶּלֶךְ ז
וּגְדֹלָיו לֵאמֹר הָאָדָם וְהַבְּהֵמָה הַבָּקָר וְהַצֹּאן

"[R' Yehoshua] went back to Elijah and said. . .'[The Messiah] lied to me! He said he would come today, but he did not come!'

"Elijah said to him, 'What he meant was, "Today, *if we but heed His call* . . ." ' "[1]

The fact that rank-and-file Jews are more likely to repent for their sins than are their leaders is reflected in the order of this and the previous one. The previous verse states, "And *the people* of Nineveh believed in God, so they proclaimed a fast and donned sackcloth, from their great to their small." Only afterwards did "the matter reached the king of Nineveh."

וַיְכַס שַׂק וַיֵּשֶׁב עַל הָאֵפֶר — **he covered himself with sackcloth and sat on ashes.**

As mentioned earlier, the king's robe represents all the trappings of royalty that instill arrogance in the hearts of rulers, and which in turn bring them to sin. The first step to be taken by a ruler who wishes to repent is to discard these negative influences represented by his royal garments. Instead, he should cover himself with sackcloth in an expression of humility.

In order to compensate for his propensity towards arrogance, he must make a greater effort to feel regret in his heart than the rest of the populace. This explains why the people donned sackcloth, but only the king of Nineveh "sat on ashes."

The obligation incumbent upon Israel's rulers to take extra steps to instill humility into their hearts is reflected by the following *mishnah*:

"What is the procedure to be followed on public fast days?"

"The Ark is taken out [of the synagogue] to the main square of the city. People then place ashes upon it, and upon the head of the *Nasi*, and upon the head of the *Av Beis Din*. All the others then place ashes upon their own heads."[2]

In reference to this *mishnah* the Sages ask the following question:

"Let also the *Nasi* and the *Av Beis Din* take ashes and place them upon their own heads. In what way do they differ, that others must place ashes upon their heads?

---

1. *Psalms* 95:7.
2. *Mishnah, Taanis* 2:1.

ashes. [7] *And [he] had it promulgated and declared throughout Nineveh, "By the counsel of the king and his nobles, the following: Man and beast, herd and flock,*

"[The answer is:] The act of disgracing oneself is not comparable to being disgraced by others."

Clearly, then, the *Nasi* and the *Av Beis Din* — as well as all other leaders — are required to take extra measures to humble themselves and thereby ensure that their repentance is sincere.

7. וַיַּזְעֵק וַיֹּאמֶר בְּנִינְוֵה מִטַּעַם הַמֶּלֶךְ — And [he] had it promulgated and declared throughout Nineveh, "By the counsel of the king

The verse alludes to *Yom Kippur*.

Whenever the term "the king" appears without further specification, it refers to God. According to this understanding, the verse stresses that the fast of *Yom Kippur* has been decreed "by the counsel of the King of kings."

וּגְדֹלָיו לֵאמֹר — and his nobles, the following:

The term "his nobles" refers to the Sages of the *Sanhedrin*. The fast of *Yom Kippur* is ascribed also to them because it is their responsibility to sanctify the new month of *Tishrei* and proclaim the onset of the New Year (*Rosh Hashanah*). As the Sages said, " 'For it is a decree for Israel, a judgment [day] for the God of Jacob'[1] — this teaches that the heavenly court of God does not convene to pass judgment [on *Rosh Hashanah*] unless the *Sanhedrin* of Israel below has passed [the law of] sanctifying the month."[2]

הָאָדָם — Man

An allusion to spiritual leaders and Torah scholars.

וְהַבְּהֵמָה — and the beast

An allusion to one who lacks Torah knowledge, as in the verse, "Behold days are coming — the word of God — when I shall sow the House of Israel and the House of Judah — the seed of *man* and the seed of *beast* (sing.)"[3]

הַבָּקָר וְהַצֹּאן — herd and flock,

People who lack Torah knowledge ("beasts") belong to either the

---

1. *Psalms* 81:5.

2. *Rosh Hashanah* 8b.

3. *Jeremiah* 31:26. See *Sotah* 22a.

אַל-יִטְעֲמוּ מְאוּמָה אַל-יִרְעוּ וּמַיִם אַל-יִשְׁתּוּ:
וְיִתְכַּסּוּ שַׂקִּים הָאָדָם וְהַבְּהֵמָה וְיִקְרְאוּ אֶל-
אֱלֹהִים בְּחָזְקָה וְיָשֻׁבוּ אִישׁ מִדַּרְכּוֹ הָרָעָה
וּמִן-הֶחָמָס אֲשֶׁר בְּכַפֵּיהֶם: מִי-יוֹדֵעַ יָשׁוּב

"herd" or the "flock."

The "herd" is the more inferior of the two categories. It is comprised of steadfast apostates called פּוֹשְׁעֵי יִשְׂרָאֵל, "the sinners of Israel."[1]

The second category — the "flock" — is comprised of people who lack the knowledge to distinguish between good and bad, but who heed the words of Torah scholars and are drawn after them. They are likened to a flock led by a shepherd. In reference to them the verse states, "You are My flock, the flock of My pasture, You are man."[2]

Israel's spiritual leaders fast on the eve of *Rosh Hashanah*, while the average person fasts during the Ten Days of Repentance between *Rosh Hashanah* and *Yom Kippur*. However, on *Yom Kippur* itself, even the "beast" of the "herd" come to synagogue to pray and fast.

אַל יִרְעוּ — they shall neither graze

Since according to our allegorical understanding the verse alludes to human beings, the words "they shall neither graze" must be interpreted accordingly.

These words are rather a figurative reference to the prohibition of working on *Yom Kippur*. Work is likened to grazing, for just as sheep graze in order to sustain themselves, so too, men work in order to earn their livelihood.

8. וְיִתְכַּסּוּ שַׂקִּים הָאָדָם וְהַבְּהֵמָה — They are to cover themselves with sackcloth — both man and beast —

"Both man and beast" — i.e., Torah scholars and ignorant individuals alike — are to humble themselves before God on this holy day of *Yom Kippur*.

---

1. See *Chullin* 5a.
2. *Ezekiel* 34:31.

3/8-9
shall not taste anything; they shall neither graze nor drink water. ⁸ They are to cover themselves with sackcloth — both man and beast — and let them call out mightily to God; each person is to turn back from his evil way, and from the robbery which is in their hands. ⁹ He who knows — let him repent

---

וְיִקְרְאוּ אֶל אֱלֹהִים בְּחָזְקָה — **and let them call out mightily to God;**

An allusion to the heartfelt prayers and supplications uttered by the Jewish People all day long on *Yom Kippur*.

וְיָשֻׁבוּ אִישׁ מִדַּרְכּוֹ הָרָעָה וּמִן הֶחָמָס אֲשֶׁר בְּכַפֵּיהֶם — **each person is to turn back from his evil way, and from the robbery which is in their hands.**

In reference to this verse the Sages said, "What does 'and from the robbery which is in their hands' mean? Shmuel said: Even if a person has stolen a beam and used it to build a tower, he dismantles the entire tower and returns the beam to its rightful owner."[1]

The verse emphasizes the importance of returning stolen objects because, as the Sages say, "*Yom Kippur* atones for transgressions between man and God, but *Yom Kippur* does not atone for transgressions between man and his fellow until [the transgressor] appeases his fellow."[2]

9. מִי יוֹדֵעַ — **He who knows —**

The words "He who knows" allude to the verse, "If a person will sin: If he accepted a demand for an oath, and he is a witness — either *he saw or he knew* — if he does not testify, he shall bear his iniquity."[3]

According to the *Zohar*, the clause "who saw or knew" alludes to a man's deliberate sins committed in full knowledge that his actions comprise a violation of God's will. If "he does not testify" — i.e., if he does not confess his sin before God — then "he must bear his iniquity" — i.e., guilt upon leaving this world.[4]

---

1. *Taanis* 16a.
2. *Yoma* 8b-9a.
3. *Leviticus* 5:1.
4. *Zohar* Volume III, 13b.

וְנִחַם הָאֱלֹהִים וְשָׁב מֵחֲרוֹן אַפּוֹ וְלֹא
נֹאבֵד: וַיַּרְא הָאֱלֹהִים אֶת־מַעֲשֵׂיהֶם כִּי־
שָׁבוּ מִדַּרְכָּם הָרָעָה וַיִּנָּחֶם הָאֱלֹהִים עַל־
הָרָעָה אֲשֶׁר־דִּבֶּר לַעֲשׂוֹת־לָהֶם וְלֹא עָשָׂה:

א וַיֵּרַע אֶל־יוֹנָה רָעָה גְדוֹלָה וַיִּחַר לוֹ:

וְשָׁב מֵחֲרוֹן אַפּוֹ וְלֹא נֹאבֵד — He will turn away from His burning wrath so that we not perish."

By refraining from eating and working, we will not perish, as it is written, "For any soul who will not be afflicted on this very day (i.e., *Yom Kippur*) will be cut off from its people. And any soul who will do any work on this very day, I will make that soul *perish* from among its people."[1]

10. וַיַּרְא הָאֱלֹהִים אֶת מַעֲשֵׂיהֶם — And God saw their deeds

God saw that they had performed all the required acts and deeds of rectification — they fasted (תַּעֲנִית), wore sackcloth (שַׂק), sat in ashes (וָאֵפֶר), wept (בְּכִי) and mourned (הֶסְפֵּד). The first letter of these five forms of penitence spell the word תְּשׁוּבָה — "repentance."[2]

כִּי שָׁבוּ מִדַּרְכָּם הָרָעָה — that they repented from their evil way;

The essential reason they were forgiven, however, was that they truly felt regret for their deeds and repented from the bottom of their hearts. This is evident from the Sages' account of the sermon that used to be delivered in their time on public fast days:

"My brothers," one of the elders would intone, "neither sackcloth nor fasting will help, but only repentance and worthy deeds, for we see that in reference to the inhabitants of Nineveh, Scripture does not say, "And God saw their *sackcloth and fasting*," but rather "And God saw their *deeds*, that they *repented* from their evil way. . ."[3]

God seals the penitent's favorable decree on *Yom Kippur*. As the Sages said, "Man is judged on *Rosh Hashanah*, and his decree is sealed on *Yom Kippur*."[4]

---

1. *Leviticus* 23:29-30.
2. *Shnei Luchos Habris*, Section II, beginning of *Rosh Hashanah* in name of *Arizal*. See *Sha'ar Ruach Hakodesh*, *Tikun* 17.
3. *Taanis* 16a.
4. *Rosh Hashanah* 16a.

3/10   *and God will be relentful; He will turn away from His burning wrath so that we not perish."*

¹⁰ And God saw their deeds, that they repented from their evil way; and God relented concerning the calamity He had said He would bring upon them and did not act.

4/1   ¹ **A**nd it displeased Jonah greatly and it grieved him.

4.

1. וַיֵּרַע אֶל יוֹנָה רָעָה גְדוֹלָה — And it displeased Jonah greatly

The verse alludes to the physical hardships experienced by the reincarnated *neshamah* of someone who had sinned in a previous life. As the Sages say, "Longevity, children and a livelihood do not depend on merit, but on *mazal*"[1] — the reincarnated *neshamah* of a person who sinned in his previous life is destined to feel deprivation in these three areas even if he is completely righteous in his present life.

This was the Sages' intention when they said that Moses asked God, "Master of the universe! Why do some righteous individuals enjoy a good life, while other righteous individuals suffer?"

God answered him, "Moses, a righteous individual who enjoys a good life is a righteous individual who was born to a righteous individual, while a righteous individual who suffers is a righteous individual who was born to a wicked individual."[2] In other words, a righteous person who was righteous in a previous life will enjoy a good life, whereas a righteous person who was wicked in a previous life will suffer throughout his next incarnation.

The Sages elaborate the concept further:

"The twenty-eight days of the moon include fourteen days when the moon is waxing, and fourteen days when the moon is waning. He who is born during the days when the moon is waxing will have children, a long life, prosperity, a livelihood, joy and peace. . . But he who is born when the moon is incomplete. . .will be lacking in all these things — he will be poor and destitute, he will lack sustenance, and he will not have children or a long life. He who is born in the middle will be an average

---

1. *Moed Katan* 28a.

2. *Berachos* 7a.

ד/ב-ג‏ ג‏ וַיִּתְפַּלֵּל אֶל־יְהוָה וַיֹּאמַר אָנָּה יְהוָה הֲלוֹא־זֶה דְבָרִי
עַד־הֱיוֹתִי עַל־אַדְמָתִי עַל־כֵּן קִדַּמְתִּי לִבְרֹחַ
תַּרְשִׁישָׁה כִּי יָדַעְתִּי כִּי אַתָּה אֵל־חַנּוּן וְרַחוּם אֶרֶךְ
ג‏ אַפַּיִם וְרַב־חֶסֶד וְנִחָם עַל־הָרָעָה: וְעַתָּה יְהוָה

---

person. And what determines whether one is born in the beginning, end, or middle? His reincarnation determines it. . .that which occurred before he came to this world."[1]

וַיִּחַר לוֹ — and it grieved him

Jonah represents the *neshamos* of righteous men who behaved wickedly in a previous lifetime and consequently had to undergo the anguish of reincarnation.

He greatly envied the people of Nineveh for meriting "two tables"[2] — an enjoyable life in this world, and a portion in the World to Come. They lived enjoyable lives in this world because they were not reincarnated souls, and they merited to a portion in the World to Come because they were swift to repent for their sins.

Rebbi felt the same way when he learned of the eternal reward that R' Eliezer son of Durdaya earned in a single moment through repentance. At this time, Rebbi cried out and declared, "Some people acquire their [portion in the] World [to Come] over many years, while others acquire their [portion in the] World [to Come] in a single moment!"[3] In other words, some people repent for their sins in time and avoid the need to be reincarnated, while others do not repent in time and as a result must suffer the agony of another incarnation before finally enjoying their eternal reward in the World to Come.

This is the deeper intention of the Sages' statement, "A *kav* of carobs is sufficent for Chanina [ben Dosa]. . ."[4] Since the carob tree first gives forth fruit seventy years after it has taken root, the one who plants it will not live long enough to enjoy its fruit in this world.[5] Likewise, righteous individuals who failed to repent for their sins in time and were

---

1. *Tikunei Zohar* 117b.
2. *Berachos* 5b. According to Vilna Gaon's commentary, the term means "this world and the World to Come."
3. *Avodah Zarah* 17a.
4. *Berachos* 17b.
5. *Taanis* 23a.

² *He prayed to* HASHEM, *and said, "Please* HASHEM, *was this not my contention when I was still on my own soil? I therefore had hastened to flee to Tarshish, for I knew that You are a gracious and compassionate God, slow to anger, abounding in kindness, and relentful of punishment.* ³ *So now,* HASHEM,

---

reincarnated will not get to enjoy the reward of their righteous deeds in this world — instead, like the planter of the carob tree, they will have to wait to reap their reward until after their death.

2. וַיִּתְפַּלֵּל אֶל ה׳ — He prayed to HASHEM

When the *neshamah* is reincarnated, it "prays to God" to provide food and other physical necessities to the body in order to alleviate its suffering.

וַיֹּאמַר אָנָּה ה׳ — and said, "Please, HASHEM..."

At this point, the reincarnated *neshamah* is confronted with the sins it committed in its previous life — when it was "still on its own soil" — and it is admonished for not having repented at an earlier stage, before it lay on its deathbed.

The reincarnated *neshamah* defends itself by claiming that it fully intended to repent for its sins, yet the knowledge that God is "gracious and compassionate" and accepts repentance even one day before a wicked person's death — as proven by Nineveh's narrow escape from destruction — caused it to "flee to Tarshish" — i.e., pursue worldly desires in its youth and postpone repentance until later in life. The *neshamah* explains that it unexpectedly fell ill, and that circumstances beyond its control prevented it from repenting fully as it had intended. As a consequence, it entered the grave still tainted by sin.

This is the intention of the Sages' statement, "Whoever says, 'I will sin and then repent, I will sin and then repent,' he will not be afforded the opportunity to repent."[1]

וְנִחָם עַל הָרָעָה — and relentful of punishment

Recognizing this Divine attribute, the reincarnated *neshamah* beseeches God for mercy.

---

1. *Yoma* 8b.

3. וְעַתָּה ה׳ קַח נָא אֶת נַפְשִׁי מִמֶּנִּי — So now HASHEM, please take my life from me,

The *neshamah* pleads with God to alleviate its suffering, and if this is not possible, to simply cut short its stay in this world. The following account illustrates this idea:

"R' Elazar ben Pedas was extremely poor and destitute. He once [let out blood] and did not have anything to eat. He found a garlic clove and put it in his mouth, and he became weak and fell senseless. His colleagues came to ask about his welfare, and they saw him crying and laughing while a spark emerged from his forehead. When he awakened, they asked him, 'Why did you laugh and cry? Why did a spark emerge from your forehead?'

"He responded, 'The Holy One, Blessed is He, was sitting with me, and I asked him, "For how long will I continue to suffer?" He replied, "Elazar, My son, would you like Me to overturn the world and create it anew so that perhaps you will be created in a time of prosperity?" I answered, "All that, and *perhaps*?" Then I asked Him, "Have I lived out most of my years, or do I have many more left?" He answered, "You have lived out most of them." At this point I said, "If so, I do not wish to have the world overturned and created anew so that I might be created in a time of prosperity." ' "[1]

According to the *Zohar*, God's suggestion, "Would you like Me to overturn the world," is not referring to the world at large, but rather, to the "small world" — i.e., a person. In essence He asked, "Would you like Me to take your life and bring you back in a different incarnation? Perhaps you will be born in a more auspicious moment."[2]

R' Elazar seriously contemplated the merits of dying and having his world overturned. He only decided against this option when he discovered that he had already lived out most of his life, and that his suffering would soon be over.

So too, the reincarnated *neshamah* prefers to die than to continue suffering.

1. *Taanis* 25a.
2. *Tikunei Zohar* 116b.

כִּי טוֹב מוֹתִי מֵחַיָּי — **for better is my death than my life."**

The *neshamah's* wish coincides with the verse, "So I consider more fortunate the dead who have already died than the living who are still alive."[1]

This verse contains two seemingly superfluous clauses: "the dead *who have already died*," and "the living *who are still alive*." Ostensibly, the verse could simply read, "I consider more fortunate the dead than the living."

The answer to this difficulty is that the verse draws a distinction between souls that are reincarnated and those that are not — "the dead" souls that "have already died" and will never again be reincarnated are more fortunate than the dead souls which are "still alive," and are brought once again to the world through reincarnation.

With this explanation, it is possible to understand the Sages' following statement:

"*Beis Shammai* and *Beis Hillel* carried on a dispute for two and a half years. These said, 'It would have been better for man not to have been created rather than to have been created,' while these said, 'It is better for man that he was created rather than not to have been created.' They counted votes and decided — 'It would have been better for man not to have been created rather than to have been created. However, now that he has been created, he must examine his deeds.' "[2]

A number of questions come to mind. For instance, how could anyone suggest that it would have been better for man not to have been created? If this were true, why would God have created man? Surely God knows what is better for man! Furthermore, why did the Sages say, "However, *now* that he has been created"? A more fitting expression would be, "However, *since* he has been created. . ." Finally, why did the Sages conclude "now that he has been created, *he must examine his deeds*"? Would it not have been more appropriate to conclude, "now that he has been created, he must *serve God and behave righteously*"?

---

1. *Ecclesiastes* 4:2.
2. *Eruvin* 13b.

ד/ד-ה ד-ה וַיֹּאמֶר יהוה הַהֵיטֵב חָרָה לָךְ: וַיֵּצֵא יוֹנָה
מִן־הָעִיר וַיֵּשֶׁב מִקֶּדֶם לָעִיר וַיַּעַשׂ לוֹ שָׁם
סֻכָּה וַיֵּשֶׁב תַּחְתֶּיהָ בַּצֵּל עַד אֲשֶׁר יִרְאֶה מַה־

The answer is that *Beis Shammai* and *Beis Hillel* were not arguing about whether or not it is better for man to have been created in the first place. Rather, their argument centered around the question of whether man benefits from being reincarnated. According to one opinion, man ultimately benefits from reincarnation because he is given the opportunity to perform additional *mitzvos* each time his *neshamah* returns to the world. The Sages concluded that "it would have been better for man not to have been created (i.e., reincarnated)" — a person must purify his *neshamah* during his life and thereby avoid having to return to this world again. This conclusion is in line with the explanation given on the verse, "I consider more fortunate the dead than the living."[1] This solves our first question.

As for our second question, the expression "*now* that he has been created" conveys that the "man" under discussion is someone whose *neshamah* had come to the world in a previous life. This person's main objective *now* — i.e., in his second incarnation — is to rectify the transgressions he committed in his previous life. For this reason the Sages said, "he must examine his deeds" — i.e., the wicked deeds he performed in his past lifetime — and not, "he should serve God and behave righteously," for the main purpose of reincarnation is not to perform additional *mitzvos*, but to rectify the transgressions one committed in a previous life.

By now, the reader is probably wondering, "How can I possibly know which transgressions I committed in a previous life? And without this knowledge, how can I determine what wrongdoings I have been sent to rectify in this reincarnation?"

There are two methods by which to discover one's past transgressions. The first consists of identifying the transgressions that one commits most frequently in one's current life; for this reason the Sages said, "he should examine his deeds." The second method consists of identifying the transgressions to which one is most attracted — their special allure stems from one's *neshamah* having become accustomed

---

1. *Ecclesiastes* 4:2.

⁴ *And HASHEM said, "Is it right of you to be so deeply grieved?"*

⁵ *Jonah left the city and stationed himself at the east of the city; he made himself a booth there, and sat under it in the shade until he would see what*

---

to these forbidden pleasures in a previous life.

4. וַיֹּאמֶר ה' הַהֵיטֵב חָרָה לָךְ — **And HASHEM said, "Is it right of you to be so deeply grieved?"**

God in essence told Jonah, "Why are you so deeply grieved by Nineveh's inhabitants?" Similarly, God asked Cain, "Why are you so annoyed and jealous [of your brother Abel]?"[1]

5. וַיֵּצֵא יוֹנָה מִן הָעִיר וַיֵּשֶׁב מִקֶּדֶם לָעִיר — **Jonah left the city and stationed himself at the east of the city;**

When the reincarnated *neshamah* of a person senses that God will not answer its prayers and extricate it from adversity, it "leaves the city" — i.e., it distances itself from all worldly affairs, and occupies itself exclusively with Torah study. This is the intention of the clause "Jonah. . .stationed himself at the east (*mikedem*) of the city" — *kedem* is also associated with the word *kodem*, "before." This is an allusion to the Torah, which was created before this world, as it is written, "God made me as the beginning of His way, before His deeds of yore."[2]

וַיַּעַשׂ לוֹ שָׁם סֻכָּה וַיֵּשֶׁב תַּחְתֶּיהָ בַּצֵּל — **he made himself a booth there, and sat under it in the shade**

The Hebrew term סֻכָּה ("booth") alludes to the festival of *Succos* (סֻכּוֹת). By examining the fundamental components of this festival, the verse can be understood in a different light.

It is written in the Torah, "You shall make the festival of *Succos* for a seven-day period, when you gather in from your threshing floor and from your wine press."[3] In addition, the Torah specifies, "But on the fifteenth day of the seventh month, when you gather in the crop of the land, you shall celebrate God's festival for a seven-day period. . ."[4]

---

1. *Genesis* 4:6.
2. *Proverbs* 8:22. See *Pesachim* 54a.
3. *Deuteronomy* 16:13.
4. *Leviticus* 23:39.

It is also written, "You shall dwell in booths for a seven-day period. . ."[1]

According to the Sages, the verse "when you gather in from your threshing floor and from your wine press" refers to the waste products of the threshing floor and of the wine press.[2] These waste products are to be used as thatching material for the booths ("*succos*") in which the Jewish People are obligated to dwell during the week-long festival of *Succos*. The Oral Law adds another specification — the roof of the booth must provide more shade than the amount of sunlight that penetrates through the thatching.

Each of these legal specifications has symbolic meaning. The sun that shines down on the booth represents all worldly affairs, for the continuing existence of the entire world depends on the sun. This is the deeper intention of the Sages' statement, "Longevity, children and a livelihood do not depend on merit, but on *mazal* (i.e., on the constellations),"[3] for as the *Zohar* states, "Even when the sun sets, it shines upon the moon, the stars and all constellations."[4] Similarly, the *Zohar* states, "The intensity of the sun produces more gold."[5]

The terms "threshing floor" and "wine press" represent bread and wine, and in a wider sense, all worldly pleasures. By commanding us to reside in booths made from the *waste products* of the threshing floor and the wine press, the Torah teaches us a deeper lesson — we must limit the extent to which we partake of worldly pleasures, and thereby prevent ourselves from falling prey to the wiles of the Evil Inclination. Instead of exposing ourselves to the glaring rays of "the sun" and pursuing wealth and physical pleasures, we are bidden to take shelter in the cool shade of the *succah* and occupy ourselves with spiritual undertakings. As the *Mishnah* states, "Make your Torah [study] a fixed practice"[6] and your labor temporary. For this reason, *Halachah* stipulates that the roof of the *succah* must provide more shade than the amount of sunlight that penetrates through the thatching — our

1. *Leviticus* 23:42.
2. *Succah* 12a.
3. *Moed Katan* 28a.
4. *Zohar* Volume III, 290a.
5. *Zohar* Volume I, 250a.
6. *Avos* 1:15.

spiritual undertakings must "overshadow" our worldly pursuits.

Jonah (i.e., the reincarnated *neshamah*) decided to separate himself from the city (this world) and dwell in the shade of Torah study and spiritual development.

עַד אֲשֶׁר יִרְאֶה מַה יִּהְיֶה — **until he would see what would occur**

Jonah waited to see whether his *mazal* would improve, hoping constantly that his star would rise. But God demonstrated to Jonah that all benefits of this world are completely illusory, as we shall see in the following passage.

6. וַיְמַן ה׳ אֱלֹהִים קִיקָיוֹן — **HASHEM, God, designated a kikayon,**

The bad *mazal* of certain individuals cannot always be changed This is evident from the incident involving R' Elazar ben Pedas — in answer to his question "For how long will I continue to suffer?" God said, "Elazar, My son, would you like Me to overturn the world and create it anew so that perhaps you will be created in a time of prosperity?"[1] If R' Elazar's *mazal* could have been changed, God would not have suggested to recreate him in some other more auspicious time.

Nevertheless, God occasionally alleviates the suffering of unfortunate individuals by granting them a share of their portion in the World to Come during their lifetime. The Sages illustrate this idea with the following episode:

"The wife of [Chanina ben Dosa, who lived in abject poverty] said to him, 'For how long will we continue suffering like this?'

"He said to her, 'What can I do?'

"She said to him, 'Ask for mercy, that they should alleviate our suffering with some of the reward that is stored away for the righteous in the World to Come.'

"[Chanina ben Dosa] asked for mercy, and the image of a hand came out and presented him with a golden table-leg. In a dream, he saw all the righteous eating upon golden tables supported by three legs, while he ate on a golden table supported by two legs.

"He said to his wife, 'Does it please you to know that all the righteous

---

1. *Taanis* 25a.

מֵעַל לְיוֹנָה לִהְיוֹת צֵל עַל־רֹאשׁוֹ לְהַצִּיל
לוֹ מֵרָעָתוֹ וַיִּשְׂמַח יוֹנָה עַל־הַקִּיקָיוֹן שִׂמְחָה
גְדוֹלָה: וַיְמַן הָאֱלֹהִים תּוֹלַעַת בַּעֲלוֹת ז

---

will eat upon golden tables supported by three legs, while we will eat on a table that is missing one of its legs?"[1]

The following episode illustrates the same idea:

"Rabbah bar Avuha found Elijah. . . He said to him, 'I am destitute.'

"[Elijah] took him and brought him into *Gan Eden*. He said to him, 'Remove your cape and gather [into it] those leaves.'

"He took and collected [the leaves]. As he was leaving, he heard a voice saying, 'Who has eaten his portion in the World to Come like Rabbah bar Avuha?'

"He emptied [his robe] and discarded [the leaves]. Even so, his robe absorbed the fragrance, and he sold it for twelve thousand *dinar*."[2]

This is the deeper intention of the verse, "HASHEM, God, designated a *kikayon*." The *kikayon* that afforded Jonah shade symbolizes the portion of the reward in store for the righteous in the World to Come which sometimes manifests itself in this world in the form of wealth. So too did the leaves that Elijah showed to Rabbah bar Avuha.

וַיַּעַל מֵעַל לְיוֹנָה לִהְיוֹת צֵל עַל רֹאשׁוֹ לְהַצִּיל לוֹ מֵרָעָתוֹ — **which rose up above Jonah to form a shade over his head to relieve him from his discomfort;**

As mentioned above, the sun represents worldly prosperity. Just as it rises at dawn, grows increasingly stronger as it reaches its zenith, and then sinks in the sky and disappears, so too, good *mazal* shines on a person for a time, but then it moves on to shine upon others. Being in the sun means to be subject to the ups and downs of this world's cycles of wealth and poverty. The shade created by the leaves of the *kikayon* represents the portion of eternal reward which God gives to certain individuals in this world to shield them from the constant fluctuations of *mazal* which are so characteristic of this transient reality.

וַיִּשְׂמַח יוֹנָה עַל הַקִּיקָיוֹן שִׂמְחָה גְדוֹלָה — **and Jonah rejoiced greatly over the** *kikayon*

---

1. *Taanis* 25a.
2. *Bava Metzia* 114b.

up above Jonah to form a shade over his head to relieve him from his discomfort; and Jonah rejoiced greatly over the kikayon.

7 Then God designated a worm at the dawn of

As mentioned earlier, the *kikayon* represents the portion of eternal reward which God gives to some unfortunate individuals in this world. Jonah, who represents the reincarnated *neshamah*, mistakenly thought that his bad *mazal* had suddenly taken a turn for the better, and that from now on he would live a comfortable life full of worldly pleasures. Little did he know that this improvement in his physical conditions was consuming his portion in the World to Come.

In reference to Jonah's *kikayon* the Sages said,

"Rabbah bar bar Chana said: I saw Jonah's *kikayon* in a vision. It resembles a barren tree; it grows in swamps; people hang it over shops (for its shade and its pleasant fragrance); oil is made from its seeds; and the ill in the Land of Israel recline under its branches."[1]

Rabbah bar bar Chana's intention was that he perceived Jonah's *kikayon* as being a symbol of opulence and wealth. "It resembles a barren tree" conveys that the *kikayon* was very large, but at the same time, ephemeral in nature. For when a person draws on his eternal reward to improve his physical conditions in this world, he transforms a self-propagating and everlasting spiritual entity into a lifeless and "barren" material substance of transient existence.

"It grows in swamps" alludes to the sordid human desire to exchange one's eternal reward for profane worldly pleasures. Ezekiel the Prophet used similar imagery to admonish the Jewish People, as it is written, "Is it not enough for you that you graze in the good pasture, that you must also trample the rest of your pasture underfoot? [Is it not enough] that you drink settled waters, that you must also befoul the rest with your feet?"[2] "People hang it over shops" alludes to the saying of the *Mishnah,* "Everything is given on collateral and a net is spread over all the living. The shop is open; the Merchant extends credit; the ledger is open; the hand writes; and whoever wishes to borrow, let him come and borrow. . ."[3] This serves as a reminder to those who enjoy a good life that

1. *Shabbos* 21a.
2. *Ezekiel* 34:18.
3. *Avos* 3:20.

הַשַּׁחַר לַמָּחֳרָת וַתַּ֣ךְ אֶת־הַקִּיקָי֖וֹן וַיִּיבָֽשׁ׃
ח וַיְהִ֣י ׀ כִּזְרֹ֣חַ הַשֶּׁמֶשׁ וַיְמַ֨ן אֱלֹהִ֜ים ר֤וּחַ קָדִים֙
חֲרִישִׁ֔ית וַתַּ֥ךְ הַשֶּׁ֛מֶשׁ עַל־רֹ֥אשׁ יוֹנָ֖ה וַיִּתְעַלָּ֑ף

---

they are paying an enormous price for these transient pleasures — they are drawing upon the spiritual riches that await them in the World to Come.

"Oil is made from its seeds" means that many wealthy people do not deserve to be wealthy, but their descendants ("seed") do. The parents accumulate wealth in order to bequeath it to their children, as in the verse, "Though he [the evil man] may amass money like dirt and prepare a wardrobe as [abundant as] clay, he may prepare, but a righteous man will wear it and a virtuous man will apportion his money."[1]

"And the ill in the Land of Israel recline under its branches" means that the purpose of wealth is to support Torah scholars, who are financially infirm. The Jews in Babylonia did not use their wealth for this purpose, as the Sages said, "The prosperous Jews of Babylonia are destined to descend into *Gehinnom* (for they do not show mercy and give charity)."[2] In contrast, the Jews living in the Land of Israel did use their wealth to support Torah scholars.

7. וַיְמַן הָאֱלֹהִים תּוֹלַעַת בַּעֲלוֹת הַשַּׁחַר לַמָּחֳרָת וַתַּךְ אֶת הַקִּיקָיוֹן וַיִּיבָשׁ — Then God designated a worm at the dawn of the morrow, and it attacked the *kikayon* so that it withered.

God destroyed the *kikayon* in order to make Jonah realize that worldly pleasures are transitory and devoid of substance.

8. וַיְהִי כִּזְרֹחַ הַשֶּׁמֶשׁ — And it happened that when the sun rose

God withdrew Jonah's eternal reward, which had temporarily shielded him from his hardship, and exposed him once again to the ruthless rays of the sun — i.e., to the constant fluctuations of *mazal* which are so characteristic of this world.

וַיְמַן אֱלֹהִים רוּחַ קָדִים חֲרִישִׁית — God designated a stifling east wind;

This was the same wind that originally struck Jonah's ship. It

---

1. *Job* 27:16-17. See *Pesachim* 49b.
2. *Beitzah* 32b.

the morrow and it attacked the kiyayon so that it withered. ⁸ And it happened that when the sun rose God designated a stifling east wind; the sun beat upon Jonah's head and he became faint;

---

represents the attribute of heavenly judgment, as explained earlier in the commentary to verse 1:4.

The wind is referred to as "stifling" because the hardship it brought upon Jonah caused him to abandon Torah study — in this sense, it "stifled" his mouth from speaking words of Torah. The "stifling" effect that hardship and adversity have on a person is alluded to in the verse, "I became mute with stillness, I was silent [even] from good, though my pain was intense"¹ — "good" refers to Torah study.

Ultimately, Jonah was left with nothing — he was robbed of all physical comforts, and he neglected his study of Torah.

וַתַּךְ הַשֶּׁמֶשׁ עַל רֹאשׁ יוֹנָה וַיִּתְעַלָּף — **the sun beat upon Jonah's head and he became faint;**

Jonah's bad *mazal* became even worse. His reaction to this turn of events is alluded to in the verse, "Though I am black with sin, I am comely with virtue, nations destined to ascend to Jerusalem; . . . Do not view me with contempt despite my swarthiness, for it is but the sin which has glared upon me. The alien children of my mother incited me and made me a keeper of the vineyards of idols, but the vineyard of my own true God I did not keep."²

Jonah — who represents the reincarnated *neshamah* — declared "though I am black" as a result of the bad *mazal* that I incurred through the sins of my previous life, "I am comely with virtue" in this life. He said, "Don't view me with contempt despite my swarthiness, for it is but the sun" of my bad *mazal* "which has glared upon me" through no fault of mine. It has glared upon me because "the alien children of my mother" — the body which my *neshamah* occupied during its first incarnation — "incited me."

In other words, Jonah's previous body persuaded his *neshamah* to focus on physical endeavors; instead of allowing his *neshamah* to

---

1. *Psalms* 39:3.

2. *Song of Songs* 1:5-6.

וַיִּשְׁאַל אֶת־נַפְשׁוֹ לָמוּת וַיֹּאמֶר טוֹב מוֹתִי
מֵחַיָּי: וַיֹּאמֶר אֱלֹהִים אֶל־יוֹנָה הַהֵיטֵב חָרָה־
לְךָ עַל־הַקִּיקָיוֹן וַיֹּאמֶר הֵיטֵב חָרָה־לִי עַד־
מָוֶת: וַיֹּאמֶר יהוה אַתָּה חַסְתָּ עַל־הַקִּיקָיוֹן
אֲשֶׁר לֹא־עָמַלְתָּ בּוֹ וְלֹא גִדַּלְתּוֹ שֶׁבִּן־לַיְלָה
הָיָה וּבִן־לַיְלָה אָבָד: וַאֲנִי לֹא אָחוּס עַל־
נִינְוֵה הָעִיר הַגְּדוֹלָה אֲשֶׁר יֶשׁ־בָּהּ הַרְבֵּה

---

pursue spiritual perfection, his body forced it to pursue worldly pleasures, which are totally alien to the *neshamah*.

Jonah in essence said, "I did not heed the warning of the verse, 'Lest strangers be sated with your strength, and your painfully earned wealth [be]in a stranger's house.'[1] Instead, my previous body 'made me a keeper the vineyards' of this world, and prevented me from guarding 'the vineyard of my own true God' — the realm of spiritual pursuits, and my portion in the World to Come. For this reason, I am now in this second life 'black' with bad *mazal*."

9. וַיֹּאמֶר אֱלֹהִים אֶל יוֹנָה הַהֵיטֵב חָרָה לְךָ עַל הַקִּיקָיוֹן — **And God said to Jonah, "Are you so deeply grieved about the *kikayon*?"**

As mentioned earlier, the *kikayon* represents worldly prosperity. God asked Jonah, "Are you so deeply grieved about the loss of your empty and meaningless worldly riches?"

וַיֹּאמֶר הֵיטֵב חָרָה לִי עַד מָוֶת — **And he said, "I am greatly grieved to death."**

Jonah confirmed his profound grief over the loss of his worldly riches. His prosperity became the central issue in his life because he abandoned Torah study. Hence, when his riches were taken away from him, he had nothing left to live for.

This is the deeper intention of the verse, "My child, do not forget My Torah, and let your heart guard My commandments, *for they add to you length of days, and years of life and peace*":[2] A person who devotes his life to Torah study feels a strong desire to live, whether in times of

---

1. *Proverbs* 5:10.

2. Ibid. 3:1-2.

4/9-11 *he asked for death saying, "Better is my death than my life!"*

⁹ And God said to Jonah, "Are you so deeply grieved about the kikayon?"

And he said, "I am greatly grieved to the point of death."

¹⁰ HASHEM said, "You took pity on the kikayon for which you did not labor, nor did you make it grow; which materialized overnight and perished overnight. ¹¹ And I — shall I not take pity upon Nineveh the great city, in which there are more

---

prosperity or deprivation. In contrast, a person who devotes his life to the amassment of wealth loses the will to live when his possessions are taken from him — he feels as though he has lost a part of his very *neshamah.*

10. וַיֹּאמֶר ה' אַתָּה חַסְתָּ עַל הַקִּיקָיוֹן אֲשֶׁר לֹא עָמַלְתָּ בּוֹ וְלֹא גִדַּלְתּוֹ שֶׁבֶּן לַיְלָה הָיָה וּבִן לַיְלָה אָבָד — HASHEM said, **"You took pity on the kikayon for which you did not labor, nor did you make it grow; which materialized overnight and perished overnight.**

God makes Jonah aware of how attached he has become to the *kikayon* despite the fact that it grew through no effort of his. On a deeper level, the verse refers to man's intense attachment to worldly pleasures despite the fact that they do not come to him as a result of his own labor, but are rather a natural consequence of his *mazal.* Man becomes attached to these pleasures even though he only enjoys them "overnight" — i.e., during his brief stay in this world.

11. וַאֲנִי לֹא אָחוּס עַל נִינְוֵה הָעִיר הַגְּדוֹלָה — And I — shall I not take pity upon Nineveh the great city,

If man can become so attached to transient pleasures, is it difficult to understand why God cherishes "that great city" — i.e., this world — which He created through His own handiwork to be His abode? It is especially dear to Him because of the existence of the Jewish People, who are called "a *great* nation."[1]

---

1. *Deuteronomy* 4:6, 4:8.

מִשְׁתֵּים־עֶשְׂרֵה רִבּוֹ אָדָם אֲשֶׁר לֹא־יָדַע בֵּין־
יְמִינוֹ לִשְׂמֹאלוֹ וּבְהֵמָה רַבָּה:

The *Haftarah* is concluded with the following verses (*Micah 7:18-20*).

מיכה יח   מִי־אֵל כָּמֹוֹךָ נֹשֵׂא עָוֹן וְעֹבֵר עַל־פֶּשַׁע
ז/יח־כ   לִשְׁאֵרִית נַחֲלָתוֹ לֹא־הֶחֱזִיק לָעַד אַפּוֹ כִּי־
יט   חָפֵץ חֶסֶד הוּא: יָשׁוּב יְרַחֲמֵנוּ יִכְבֹּשׁ עֲוֹנֹתֵינוּ
כ   וְתַשְׁלִיךְ בִּמְצֻלוֹת יָם כָּל־חַטֹּאתָם: תִּתֵּן
אֱמֶת לְיַעֲקֹב חֶסֶד לְאַבְרָהָם אֲשֶׁר־נִשְׁבַּעְתָּ
לַאֲבֹתֵינוּ מִימֵי קֶדֶם:

אֲשֶׁר יֶשׁ־בָּהּ הַרְבֵּה מִשְׁתֵּים עֶשְׂרֵה רִבּוֹ אָדָם אֲשֶׁר לֹא יָדַע בֵּין יְמִינוֹ לִשְׂמֹאלוֹ
וּבְהֵמָה רַבָּה — in which there are more than one hundred and twenty
thousand men who do not know their right from their left, and many
beasts [as well]?"

The "great city" contains two distinct groups of people:

"Men" refers to Torah scholars and to the righteous, while "beasts"
refers to people of limited Torah knowledge and fear of God.[1] Since the
Jewish People comprise 600,000 elemental souls, the ratio of Torah
scholars (120,000) to ignorant people is one-to-five. This ratio complies

---

1. See commentary on verse 3:7.

4/11 than one hundred and twenty thousand men who do not know their right from their left, and many beasts [as well]?"

The *Haftarah* is concluded with the following verses (*Micah* 7:18-20).

Micah7/ ¹⁸Who, O God, is like You, Who pardons iniquity,
7/18-20 and overlooks transgressions for the remnant of His heritage? He has not retained His wrath eternally, for He desires kindness. ¹⁹ He will again be merciful to us; He will suppress our iniquities; and cast into the depths of the sea all their sins. ²⁰ Grant truth to Jacob, kindness to Abraham, as You swore to our forefathers from ancient times.

---

with the Sages' interpretation of the verse, "I have my own vineyard; the thousand are yours, O Solomon, and two hundred to guard the fruit"[1] — of every thousand warriors that were sent out to battle by King Solomon, two hundred remained behind and studied Torah.[2]

These righteous men "do not know their right from their left" — they serve God with both their Good and Evil Inclination, as in the verse, "You shall love God your God with *all your heart*."[3]

---

1. *Song of Songs* 8:12.

2. *Shavuos* 31.

3. *Deuteronomy* 6:5.

אדרת אליהו
על ספר יונה

The Hebrew text of

Aderes Eliyahu
on Yonah

The Vilna Gaon's commentary
from which this commentary was adapted

ענין הנביא רומז על נשמת האדם. כמ״ש בזהר ועניינו ששולחה אל העוה״ז
לתקן את העולם. ולא די שלא תיקן אלא קלקל א״ע ג״כ אח״כ שולח אל
גלגול שני לתקן ותיקן אבל בצער על רוע מזלו כמ״ש לקמן:

א

א. ויהי דבר ה' אל יונה. ויהי זו היא שהשם משלח את הנשמ' לעוה״ז ואומר
לה זילי בגוף פלניא ועבד רעותי כמ״ש בזהר. יונה זו היא הנשמה כמ״ש בזוהר
שהיא כיונה פותה אין לב ועוד טעם אחר כמ״ש (בשבת דף מ״ט) מה יונה כנפיה
מגינות כו'. ועוד שאינה מנחת בן זוגה כו' וכך נקרא' בשה״ש. יונתי תמתי. ועוד
שנמסרת לשחיטה ואינה מפרכסת כמ״ש במדרש. מה המכות האלה וכו' לפיכך
נקרא' יונה בין בגלגול ראשון בין בגלגול שני בין בטובה ובין להיפך: **בן אמתי.**
בן להקב״ה שהוא אמתי כמ״ש בנים אתם לה' אלהיכם וכה״א בזוהר כמה דאית
אב לגוף כן אית אב לנשמה כו'. וחותמו של הקב״ה אמת. וכן אמרו (יומא דף
ס״ט) ורבנן היכי סמכי בדעתיהו ועקרי מה דאמר משה א״ר יצחק יודעין
בהקב״ה שאמתי הוא לפיכך לא כזבו בו: **לאמר.** כל מה שאמר לו ה' יאמר הכל
לישראל שידעו למה זה באו לעולם שיתקנו כ״א וא' א״ע וגם כל העולם: **ב. קום**
לך. קום ממקומך שישבת בג״ע ולך על העוה״ז: **נינוה.** הוא עוה״ז שהוא הדום
רגליו ושם נוהו כמ״ש בשבונו אל נוהו וכאן הוא עיקר דירתו וע״ז שלוח את
האדם לתקן את נוהו של השם: **העיר הגדולה.** ידוע שהאדם נקרא עולם קטן
ונקרא עיר קטנה כמ״ש בקהלת אם כן העולם נקרא עיר גדולה: **וקרא עליה.**
למוד את האדם דעת שישובו מדרכם הרעה כמ״ש קול או' קרא כו': **כי עלתה**
רעתם לפני. שהמקטרגים שנולדו מעונותיה' עומדים לפני וצועקים ומקטרגים
והוא טומאת המקדש וז״ש קץ כל בשר בא לפני כמ״ש בזוהר פ' ויחי: **ג. ויקם**
יונה לברוח. כמ״ש בזהר שדעתו לברוח מהשם וע״ז כשהאדם נקרא בעל
תשובה ואמר שובו אלי כו': **תרשישה.** אחר תאות עוה״ז לעשרה כמ״ש
(יחזקאל כ״ז) תרשיש סחורתך מרוב כל הון כו'. ואמר (שם) אניות תרשיש
שרותיך מערבך ותמלאי כו' ששם כל הכסף והזהב: **מלפני ה'.** שקודם בואו
לעולם עומד לפני השם כמ״ש בזהר ע״פ חי ה' אשר עמדתי לפניו וכן אחר בואו
לעוה״ב אם עובד ה' כמ״ש הנ״ל אבל הוא בורח מלפניו כמ״ש ויצא קין
מלפני ה': **וירד יפו.** שירד על העוה״ז כמ״ש על עץ הדעת שהוא דמיון עוה״ז
כידוע נחמד למראה כו'. וכן כל יפה נאמר על תאות הגופניות כמ״ש יפ״ת:
וימצא אניה. הוא הגוף מלשון תאניה ואניה. כמ״ש כל ימיו כעס ומכאובים וכן
אדם לעמל יולד כו' ועניינו כי העולם הזה דומה לים ועוה״ז ג״ע דומה ליבשה
שכל ענין יורדי הים אינם יורדים להשתקע שם אלא להביא סחורה ליבשה. וכן
נמשל עוה״ז לים וצרות עוה״ז לגלים כמ״ש כל משבריך וגליך כו' אמר אפפוני
מים כו'. וגוף דומה לספינה שע״י יורדים לים כן הנשמה ע״י הגוף באה בעוה״ז באה
לעוה״ב: **באה.** לשון נקבה לפי שהנשמה בעל של הגוף כמ״ש במדרש הנעלם
על אברהם ושרה. ולכן אצל יונה אמר ל' זכר: **תרשיש.** שמצא חומר כמותו
מוכן אל תאות עוה״ז. וע״ז כ' שלמה משלי על אשת חיל שהוא מוכן
לעבודת אלהים. וע״ז אמר מצא אשה מצא טוב. וכן מגנה אשה רעה שהוא חומר

מוכן במזגיו לרע כמ"ש: **ויתן שכרם.** ששעבד את שכלו בכוחותיו ותאותיו המגונים להחבירות בהם את הגוף וזהו שכר מה שעושה עבירות שנהנה ממנו כמ"ש בח"ה ועל זה אמרו ושכר עבירה כנגד הפסדה. וזה שאמרו רז"ל שנתן שכר כל הספינה שכל אברי הגוף נהנין מן העבירה ולכך חכמת המסכן בזויה פי' שאין האברי' נשמעין ליצר טוב מפני שיצר הרע או' לו שמח בחור בילדותך דהיינו תיכף ויצ"ט אומר ודע כי על כל אלה וכו' וזהו אתנן זונה ועז"א אמר שלמה והנה אשה לקראתו שית זונה וכו': **וירד בה.** שירד אל הגוף ויירידה גדולה היא לו מאיגרא רמה לבירא עמיקתא: **לבא כו' תרשישה.** שהגוף שהוא עיר קטנה ואנשים בה מעט שהם כוחות הגוף המגדל והמתאוה והמתעוררת ושאר כוחות הגוף וכל האברים שבו כולם לתרשיש כנ"ל: **מלפני ה'.** שכולם בורחין מלפניו ואין רוצים לפניו לעמוד: **ד. וה'.** הוא ובית דינו: **הטיל רוח גדולה.** היא מדת הדין המקטרגת לפניו תמיד ועומדת תמיד וצועקת ותטמא מקדשי וכשאדם ניתן ח"ו ברשותו אז השם משליחו על העולם הזה מלפניו ואז יורד ונטל נשמה והוא נקרא רוח כמ"ש רוח סערה כו' ונקרא גדולה שהקליפה גדולה וכל הצדיקים נקראים קטן כיעקב אבינו כמ"ש בחולין (דף ס') וכן הקדושה אזעירת גרמא כו' כמ"ש בזוהר על פסוק אל תראוני שאני שחרחורת וחרבא דמ"ה היא הלילית שמפתה את האדם ואחר כך לוקחת הנשמה והיא טיפת מרה התלויה בחרבא שממונה מת. כמ"ש (בע"ג דף כ') ועז"א אמר שלמה (משלי ה') כי נפת תטופנה שפתי זרה כו' ואחריתם מרה כלענה חדה כחרב פיות. שתי פיות בעוה"ז ובעוה"ב נוקמת ממנו לכן אמר גדולה ל' נקבה: **אל הים.** הוא עוה"ז שנמשלת לים ועוה"ב ליבשה ולכך (תמיד דף ל"ב) שאל אלכסנדרוס מוקדון את זקני הנגב בימא יאי למידר או ביבשתא א"ל ביבשתא שכל נחותי ימא לא מתבא דעתייהו עד דסלקין ליבשתא ועניינו לפי שהיה לו כל תאוות עוה"ז. ומלך על כל העולם חשב כבר ששך שאמר לרבא (ע"ג דף ס"ה) אית לכו כה"ג לעלמא דאתי. והשיב לו דידן עדיפי טפי מהאי את עליכו אימתא וכו' פי' ששאל בר ששך איזה יותר יותר טוב העוה"ז בשלוותא או העוה"ב והראה מחוש שעוה"ב טוב יותר כי טובת עוה"ב א"א להשיג לחוש וע"כ אין טובתו מפורש בכתוב ע"כ הוכיח מזה שעוה"ז אפילו אם יהיה כל העולם שלו מ"מ כל ימיו מכאובים מרבה נכסים מרבה דאגה וכבר האריכו ספרי מוסר כי אין בטוח האדם לא ברוב עשרו לא בבניו ובבנותיו ואין אדם מת מת וחצי תאוותו בידו שכל מי שיש לו יותר מתאווה ליותר משא"כ עולם הבא שבטוח שלא יקחו ממנו ונתקררה דעתו שם בחלקו. וז"ש אנן לא מהוי עלן אימתא כו'. ולכן אמר עוה"ב אין בו קנאה ושנאה כו', ולכך קרא צדיק שמת נח נפשיה ולכן אמרו יפה שעה אחת של קורת רוח בעוה"ב כו' ולכן אמרו שכל נחותי ימא כו'. **ויהי** **סער גדול בים.** שנקרא סער גדול שסוער את הים העוה"ז וכאן בלשון זכר שמתחלה באה היא אל הגוף ומחלה אותו בחלאים רעים שהיא נקראת חולה כמ"ש בקהלת ואחר כך בא ליטול נשמה על ידה כמו שבתחלה שכל הפתויים עושה ע"י כן בסוף כמ"ש בזוהר ולכן אמרו בפר"א ובמ"ר שכל הרוח והסער לא היה אלא על אותו ספינה שכל הספינות הולכין בשלום כו' וע"ש: **והאניה חשבה**

להשבר. הגוף חושב שע״כ ישבר עתה כמש״ש בזוהר שכל ימי חושב שכל העוה״ז היא שלו ולעולם לא ימות אבל עכשיו רואה ומתחיל להזכיר שע״כ ימות עכשיו והנשמה שאף שע״כ תסבול עונותיו מ״מ לא יאבד לנצח שיתוקן בגלגול כמ״ש פעמים ושלש עם גבר כו׳ משא״כ הגוף שאינו מתוקן בגלגול תשבר לנצח והוא דומה לכ״ח הצריכין שבירה ואמרו כיון שנשבר שוב אין לו תקנה ומדוייק לשון חשבה שאינו שייך על הספינה ממש: **ה. וייראו המלחים.** הם המנהיגים הגוף הם המוח והלב ושאר הכוחות: **ויזעקו איש אל אלהיו.** שצעקו ופנו אל כסף וזהב שעבדו אותם כל ימיהם שהן נקראו אלהי כסף ואלהי זהב כמ״ש המגי׳ ע״פ ביום ההוא ישליך איש את אלילי כספו. כספם בחוצות ישליכו כי לא יועילו הון ביום עברה. וכן כתוב הבוטחים על חילם כו׳: **ויטילו את הכלים אשר באניה אל הים.** י״ל כפשוטו שזורק מעל הגוף בגדים ונופל על המטה: **להקל מעליהם.** מעל האיברים שבבגדיו כבודין עליו ומניח אפילו בגדיו בעוה״ז וז״ש אל הים להקל מעלין גז״ד הקשה וז״ש אל הים או אומר ויטילו שנותן בגדיו לצדקה וז״ש אל הים להקל מעליהם את גז״ד הקשה להקל מעליו: **וינה ירד אל ירכתי הספינה.** שירד הספינה הנשמה אל הרגלים כמ״ש (בתיקון כ׳) על ותשכב מרגלותיו: **וישכב וירדם.** ששוכב על המטה ותרדמה נופלת עליו כידוע ביום המיתה וכה״א ויהי השמש לבא ותרדמה נפלה כו׳ שהוא שקיעת החמה באור הנשמה כמ״ש (בשבת דף קנ״א) עד אשר לא תחשך השמש והאור שהוא סילוק הנשמה ותרדמה נפלה על אברם שהוא הנשמה וכן נקרא ספינה שהיא קרובה אל היבש׳ אבל למעלה אמר אניה מפני שהיה הגוף על בוריו באמצע הים שהיא עוה״ז נקרא אניה כמ״ש (משלי ל׳) דרך אניה בלב ים: **ו. ויקרא אליו רב החובל.** הוא ראש המנהיגים והוא הלב: **ויאמר לו מה לך נרדם.** כמו שהביא בזוהר דלית עדן הוא כו׳: **קום קרא אל אלהיך.** להנשמה אומר קום כו׳ שממנו חוצבת: **אולי יתעשת אלהים לנו ולא נאבד.** כי הנשמה אפשר לתקן משא״כ הגוף ועם כל השייכים אליה הנפש ורוח הבהמות בגלגלו לנצח יאבדו: **ז. ויאמרו איש אל רעהו.** הכוחות והאברים אומרים זה לזה: **לכו ונפילה גורלות בשלמי הרעה הזאת לנו.** רצונם לידע ע״י חטא של מי יצא הגז״ד אם בחטא הלשון או המעור או שאר האברים: **ויפילו גורלות.** שבררו את הדבר ופשפשו: **ויפול הגורל על יונה.** על הנשמה כי כשהיא טובה אז היא מהפכת את כל הגוף לטובה אף שבעצמו חומר מזוג רע כמ״ש (משלי ו׳) איש און שהיה הנשמה שנקרא איש. הולך עקשות פה קורץ בעיניו. וכן אמרו באבות לב טוב שהוא משכן הנשמה כולל הכל: **ח. ויאמרו אליו הגידה נא לנו באשר למי הרע הזאת לנו.** מי יענש עמך איזה אבר ואיזה כח ונפש: **מה מלכתך.** מה אומנות נתן לך ה׳ כשהשלח אותך לנו: **ומאין תבא.** ומאיזה מקום חוצבת שע״כ צריך לעשות מעשים שיחזור לשרשו ולא מעסקי עוה״ז כלל: **מה ארצך.** מאיזה הארץ יצאת לכאן כמ״ש בזוהר לעבדה ולשמרה במ״ע ול״ת אם אם ארץ החיים שמשם יצאת ולשם ישוב. ואי מזה עם עתה. שכל ימיו לא הלך בדרך ישראל וגם בישראל כמה שמקצתה באים מערב רב ועמלקים כמ״ש בזוהר וכן (כמ״ש במדרש הנעלם) לך לך מארצך דא ג״ע דלתתא וכנגדו מה ארצך. וממולדתך וכנגדו מאין תבא.

ומבית אביך וכנגדו ואי זה כו'. אל הארץ אשר אראך פי' ששם אראך מה לעשות וכנגדו מה מלאכתך: **ט. ויאמר עברי אנכי.** כמ"ש בזוהר ע"פ בעבר הנהר ישבו אבותיכם וכן יי"ל על ג"ע שמלמעלה ששמש הכבוד משם חוצבת שהוא מעבר הנהר דינו' כידוע שצריך לעבור בו קודם וזו תשובה על ב' שאלות: **ואת אלהי השמים אני ירא.** זו היא מלאכתי. וזו תשובה על מה מלאכתך: **אשר עשה את הים ואת היבשה.** העוה"ז והעוה"ב וג"ע להכין בים ליבשה וזו היא תשובה על מה ארצך: **י וייראו האנשים יראה גדולה ויאמרו אליו מה זאת עשית לנו.** למה עשית כדברים האלה עד הנה אם לכך נוצרת וגדלה מעלתך: **כי ידעו האנשים כי מלפני ה' הוא בורח.** כל ימיו לכך יראו כ"ב ושאלו אותו למה עשית זאת ומנין ידעו כי בורח הוא **כי הגיד להם.** כל ימיו שכל דעתו ומגמתו לכך תמיד: **יא. ויאמרו אליו מה נעשה לך וישתוק הים מעלינו.** ומה נוכל למצוא תקנה לך שנוכל להתרפא ולהשקט מגז"ד: **כי הים הולך וסוער.** כי תמיד החולי מתגבר: **יב. ויאמר אליהם שאוני והטילוני אל הים.** כמו (בראשית מ') ישא פרעה את ראשך מעליך כי הנשמה ברגלים וצריך לעלות אל הגרון ויטילו אותו מן הספינה שהוא הגוף אל הים העוה"ז וישאר הגוף בלעדו: **וישתוק הים מעליכם.** אז לא תסבלו שום צער עוה"ז: **כי יודע אני כי בשלי הסער הגדול הזה עליכם.** כי כל קטרוג מדת הדין אינו אלא עד חיי האדם. כמ"ש בזוהר דכל תיאובתא לרוחא כו' ואין להם שום תקנה אחרת: **יג. ויחתרו האנשים.** הם כל הכוחות הנ"ל: **להשיב אל היבשה.** שרצו לילך בדרך הטובה בדרך עץ החיים: **ולא יכלו כי הים הולך וסוער.** עכשיו אין התשובה מועלת הואיל וכבר נגזרה עליו גזרה גזרה כמ"ש (ש"א ב') כי חפץ ה' להמיתם כאן לאחר גמר דין: **יד. ויקראו אל ה' ויאמרו אנא ה' אל נא נאבדה בנפש האיש הזה.** שצעקו אל ה' שאל יאבדו עם הנשמה: **ואל תתן דם נקי.** כי אתה ה' כאשר חפצת עשית. דבשלמא הנפש שהיא חצובה ממקום קדוש מהעליונים אבל החומר מזגו רע מה אנחנו חייבין אתה עשית את החומר כרצונך ממקום מטונף ובזה מרומז ברכת הנשים שעשני כרצונו שהוא משל אל החומר כנ"ל וכן דרשו בתנחומא ונפש כי תחטא כו' מלה"ד לשני ב"א אחד קרתני וא' בן שלטין ראה שניהם חטאו חטא א' פנה לקרתני כו': **טו. וישאו את יונה ויטילוהו אל הים.** שפרשה מהם הנשמה שהולכת מכל אבר ואבר אז יעמוד הים מזעפו: **טז. וייראו האנשים יראה גדולה את ה'.** שהנשמה הולכת מקודם ואח"כ פורשין הכוחות ואז קורא התרנגול כמ"ש בזוהר על מי לא יראון מלך הגוים כו' (ירמי' י'). ואז מגידים לו דין כל מעשה ומקבל על עצמו כמ"ש (עירובין דף יט) יפה דנת כו': **ויזבחו זבח לה' וידרו נדרים.** כמ"ש (שם) שלא כמדת הקב"ה כו' אדם מתחייב הריגה כו' ולא עוד אלא כאלו מקריב קרבן שנא' ולך ישולם נדר וזהו ויזבחו:

ב

א. וימן ה' דג גדול לבלוע את יונה. הוא הקבר והוא המלאך דומה שממונה על המתים כידוע ולכן נקרא דומה ששם הדומים כמ"ש לא המתים יהללו יה כו': **ויהי יונה במעי הדגה שלשה ימים ושלשה לילות.** כי כל ג' ימים הראשונים

רוצה הנשמה לירד בתוך הגוף שוכנת עליו תמיד ואח"כ כיון שרואה שנשתנה זיוויי שבקא ליה כמ"ש בירושלמי ונבקע מעיו וטורפין לו הפרש על פניו כמ"שרז"ל: **ב. ויתפלל יונה אל ה' אלהיו.** שצועק אל ה' כמ"ש (בעירובין שם) עוברי בעמק הבכא כו': **ממעי הדגה.** לשון נקבה שדומה מוסרו אח"כ לגהנם והיא נוקבא כמ"ש בזוהר. וז"ש בפרקי דר"א שפלטו דג זכר ובלעו דג נקבה והוו בו שס"ה אלפים רבו דגים קטנים כי ידוע שקליפת נוגה רמ"ח מלאכין קדישין מימינא ושס"ה שדין משמאלא. בעת **ג. ויאמר קראתי מצרה לי אל ה' ויענני.** בעת שהי' לי צרה בעוה"ז היית עונה לי ועכשיו מבטן שאול שועתי שהוא הגהנם והן בבטנה כמ"ש (איוב כ) חיל בלע ויקיאנו מבטנו יורישנו אל: **שועתי שמעת קולי.** כמ"ש (שם כ"ו) שאול ערו' נגדו ע"כ בקשתי שתענני עכשיו ה' ג"כ: **ד. ותשליכני מצולה.** במצולת חושך ששם נדונין ומשם יצרוף ויוצללו חטאתם כמ"ש (מיכה ז) תשליך במצולות ים כל כו': **בלבב.** שהוא במעמקי הארץ ים העוה"ז: **ונהר יסבבני.** כמ"ש (איוב כ"ב) ונהר יוצק יסודם שנהר דינו שופר על ראשן של רשעים כמ"ש במסכת חגיגה (פ"ב) וכן אמרו בעירובין שאמר ה' לגיהנם אני מלמעלה ואתה מלמטה כו': **כל משבריך וגליך עלי עברו.** שכבר סבלתי כל הצרות ועונשים וכל הקליפות נוטל כל א' ממנו חלקו: **ה. ואני אמרתי נגרשתי מנגד פניך.** כמו אותן שאין להם חלק לעולם הבא שהן לא חיים ולא נדונין: **אך אוסיף להביט אל היכל קדשך.** כמ"ש נשבעה בטוב ביתך כיון שראיתי שצרפתני בכור הגיהנם ע"כ לא עשה אלה כדי להביאני נקי לעולם הבא: **ו. אפפוני מים עד נפש.** כמ"ש ביון מצולה שהוא הגיהנם באתי במעמקי כו' כי באו מים כו': **תהום יסבבני.** כמ"ש (במ"ר בראשית פ' ל"ג) שהרשעים נידונים בתהום כמה מכסין במה הגיגית כו' כמ"ש (יחזקאל ל"א) ביום רדתו שאולה האבלתי כסתי עליו את תהו' הובלתי רשעים לגהנם וכסיתי עליהם את התהום: **סוף חבוש לראשי.** כמ"ש (איוב כ"ח) קץ שם לחשך ולכל תכלית הוא חוקר אבן אפל וצלמות שאמרו על הלילית שהוא חרבא דמ"ה והוא סוף לכל אדם סופא דכל דרגין כמ"ש בזוהר. ואמרו (סוטה דף ג) כל העושה עבירה מלפפתו ומוליכתו כו' קשורה בו ככלב ופרשו שקאי עליה וזה אמרו סוף כו': **ז. לקצבי הרים ירדתי.** כמ"ש (בחגיגה פ"ב) הארץ על מה עומדת על המים. מים על הרים והן אבני בהו שהמשוקעות בתהום ושם ירד בתהום והם ד' קליפין שבהן הרשעים נידונים כמ"ש בזוהר והן מסודרין בפ' בראשית תהו ובהו וחושך ותהום ר"ל. ואמרו (בחגיגה פ"ב) תהו זה קו ירוק והוא קץ הבשר הנ"ל טפה של מרה שממנה פניו מורירקות כמ"ש (ירמיה ל') ונהפכו כל פנים לירקון שמזעף כל העולם כולו כנ"ל ואמרו שממנו יוצא חושך לעולם שמחשיך כל הבריות וזהו מ"ש סוף חבוש כו' וכנגד בהו כו' לקצבי הרים כו'. וכנגד חשך כו' ותשליכני מצולה כו' וכנגד תהום אמר תהום יסובבני: **הארץ בריחיה בעדי לעולם.** כמ"ש (איוב ז') כן ירד שאול לא יעלה אך זאת אני מפרש **ותעל משחת חיי ה' אלהי:ח. בהתעטף עלי נפשי את ה' זכרתי.** עכשיו מתחיל להזכיר מקצת מע"ט שעשה קודם מותו שאע"פ שאין תשובתו מקובלת כ"כ מ"מ מועיל לי להעלות אחר שיסבול הכל מגיהנם כידוע ואמר מ"מ בהיות נפשו עטופה בחולי פני אל ה' ואע"פ שמחמת

דוחקי מ"מ ה' ברוב רחמיו תשב אנוש עד דכא וזה אמר **ותבא אליך תפלתי אל**
היכל קדשך: ט. משמרים הבלי שוא. לא כאותם ששומרים את ממונם כמ"ש
(תהלים ל"ט) אך הבל יהמיין יצבור כו' וכ"א קהל' ושנאתי כל עמלי כו' שאניחנו
כו' גם זה הבל כו' כ"ש בשעת גניתתו שהוא הבלי שוא לריק: **חסדם יעזבו.** כי
ניתן המעות לאדם לעשות חסד שאינו עליו אלא כגבאי ואף במיתתו מ"מ יעזוב
מעשות החסד ממה שניתן לו: **י. ואני בקול תודה.** כמ"ש ועתה תנו תודה לה'
(עזרא י') ששבו בוידוי דברים: **אזבחה לך.** כמ"ש (ביומא פ"ח) בא וראה כו'
ומקבלין אותו ולא עוד אלא שדומה כמקריבין קרבן שנאמר ונשלמה פרים כו'
אוהבם נדב': **אשר נדרתי אשלמה.** שחלקתי צדקה: **ישועתה לה'.** שכל ימי
החולי צפיתי ישועתה לה' עכשיו מבקש שתעלני: **יא. ויאמר ה' לדג.** אומר
למלאך דומה שיחזור לה' הנשמה ויקיא כמ"ש (איוב ב') חיל בלע ויקיאנו: **את**
יונה אל היבשה. לג"ע כנ"ל:

ג

א. ויהי דבר ה' אל יונה שנית. ששולח אותו בגלגול לתקן עותתו: **ב. קום לך**
אל נינוה העיר הגדולה וקרא אליה את הקריאה. הידוע לך כבר: **אשר אנכי**
דובר אליך. שדברתי לך כבר: **ג. ויקם יונה וילך אל נינוה כדבר ה'.** שהלך לא
כפעם הראשון אלא לקיים דבר ה': **ונינוה היתה עיר גדולה.** כנ"ל: **לאלהים**
מהלך שלשה ימים. שעקרו של אדם להתהלך לפני אלהים תמיד כמ"ש בכל
הצדיקים אבל נינוה לא הלכו לפני אלהים אלא רק ג' ימים והם ר"ח אלול
בהתראה ראשונה ור"ה ויו"כ וכתבו הסי' ארי"ה שאג מי לא יירא כמ"ש (עמוס
ב') היתקע שופר בעיר ועם לא יחרדו מכאן ואילך כיון דדש דש. וא"ל דלכך
מפסיקין לתקוע לער"ה דבל' יום כיון דדש נעשה טבע כמ"ש אצל טיטוס:
ד. ויחל יונה לבוא בעיר מהלך יום אחד. ביום א' שהתחיל להלוך והוא בר"ח
אלול להוכיח אותם: **ויאמר עוד מ' יום.** יש פנאי לשוב עד יוה"כ: **ונינוה**
נהפכת. שאז נחתם אם לא ישובו: **ה. ויאמינו אנשי נינוה באלהים ויקראו**
צום. הן בעשי"ת כמ"ש במדרש שהבינונים מתענים: **וילבשו שקים מגדולם**
ועד קטנם. כמו שנהגו בימים קדמונים בימי הצום: **ו. ויגע הדבר אל מלך נינוה.**
בו יותר מאחרים שממנו יתחילו (כמ"ש ר"ה פ"ק) מלך נכנס תחלה לדין. ועי"ז
מיושב הירושלמי (ר"ה פ"ק) בקדמייתא בהיל ולא בהיל כיון דתקע תנינו' בהיל
ואמר השתא ודאי אתי משיח והוא תמוה מאד. ונ"ל כי ענין התקיעות ב"פ א'
להזהיר את הגדולים שהם נכנסי' תחלה לדין. והשנית להזהיר את כל העם והוא
מרומז (במדבר י') ותקעו בהן ונועדו אליך כל העדה. כי אמר ה' ית' בתחלה עשה
לך שתי חצוצרות כו' כי בר"ה שתי חצוצרות מן הצדדין והיו לך למקרא העדה
להזהיר אותם ותקעו בהן ונועדו אליך כו' זו בכל התקיעות ואם באחת יתקעו
בפעם ראשון ונועדו אליך הנשיאים ראשי אלפי ישראל: **ויקם מכסאו ויעבר**
אדרתו מעליו. גאותו וגאונו: **ויבס שק וישב על האפר.** לכך בפעם הראשון לא
בהיל כ"כ שבעלי גאוה אינם מוכנים כ"כ לעשות תשובה מחמת רוב גאותם
ועדונם וכ"כ שמקודם ויאמינו אנשי כו' ואח"כ ויגע הדבר כו' והוצרך לקום
מכסאו ולהסיר אדרתו היא הגאוה ובו כל מדות הרעות ואח"כ ויכס שק כו'

והוצרך לעשות הכנעה יותר מהם וישב על האפר וכ"א בתענית ונתן בראש
הנשים ואמרו רז"ל שאין דומה המתבייש מעצמו כו' אבל בפעם שבא להזהיר
את דלת העם שהם מוכנים לתשובה בהיל אמר השתא אתי משיח ודאי כמ"ש
בחלק היום אם בקולי תשמעו: **ז. ויזעק ויאמר בנינוה מטעם המלך.** מלך סתם
הוא היית"ש: **וגדוליו לאמר.** הם שקבעו ר"ה כמ"ש אין ב"ד של מעלה כו' עד
שב"ד שלמטה מקדשין כו': **האדם.** הם הגדולים והת"ח: **והבהמה.** הם ע"ה)
כמ"ש (בחולין דף ה') ע"פ וזרעתי את ב"י זרע אדם וזרע כו' קא חלקי קרא זרע
אדם וזרע בהמה לחוד: **הבקר והצאן.** כי יש בעו"הז שני מיני א' בהמה
גסה והם פושעי ישראל (כמ"ש שם) מן הבהמה להביא ב"א שדומין לבהמה
מכאן אמרו כו' ומין הב' בהמה דקה והם אינם יודעים בין טוב לרע אבל הן
נמשכין אחר ת"ח ושומעין לדבריהם ונמשכים כצאן אחר רועה ועליהן אמר
הכתוב (יחזקאל ל"ד) ואתן צאני צאן מרעיתי: **אל יטעמו מאומה אל ירעו.**
שלא ילכו כל היום אחר פרנסה כלל: **ומים אל ישתו.** כמ"ש ביוה"כ כולם
מתענים הש"י מוחל כו': **ח. ויתכסו שקים האדם והבהמה.** כנ"ל: **ויקראו אל**
ה' בחזקה. שצועקים כל היום בבקשות גדולות ובתחנונים: **וישובו איש מדרכו**
הרעה ומן החמס אשר בכפיהם. כמ"ש בתענית אפי' גזל כו' ואמרו עבירות
שבין אדם למקום יו"כ כו' עד שירצה כו': **ט. מי יודע כו'.** כמ"ש או ראה או ידע:
ישוב ונחם אלהים ושב מחרון אפו ולא נאבד כו'. כמ"ש (ויקרא כ"ג)
והאבדתי את הנפש כו': **י. וירא אלהים את מעשיהם.** שעשו כל התיקונים שק
ואפר כו' ר"ת תשובה ועיקר כי שבו מדרכם הרעה כמ"ש בתענית פ"ד: **וינחם**
האלהים על הרעה אשר דבר לעשות להם. ולא עשה וחתם אותו לטובה:

ד

א. וירע אל יונה רעה גדולה. שהרע לו מאד בחוסר מזונות ושאר דברים.
והענין כי בני חיי ומזוני לא בזכותא תליא מילתא כו' ואמרו (ברכות פ"ק) צדיק
וטוב לו צדיק בן צדיק כו' והענין כמ"ש בזוהר כי מי שהיה בגלגול ראשון רע וזה
צדיק בן רשע מורידו הש"י בחסרון הלבנה שאין השמש זורחת נגדה כי כל
מעשה עו"הז הכל משמש והירח בקבלותא מהשמש כמ"ש (תהלים קל"ו)
לממשלת היום כו' ואז הוא בחסרון כל ימיו אע"פ שהוא צדיק גמור עכשיו: **ויחר**
לו. שקינא באנשי ננוה שזכו לב' שולחנו' בחייהם וע"ז בכי רבי ואמר יש קונה
עולמו בשעה א' ששב בחייו כו' ויש קונה בע' שנה ולא יזכה אלא בעו"ה"ב וזהו
וחנינא בני די דיו בקב חרובין. כי חרובין אינם אוכלים מפירותיו אלא לאחר
שבעים שנה. כמ"ש אצל חוני המעגל לכך ניזון בקב כו' והכל שקלקלו בגלגול
הראשון כמ"ש בזוהר דאפריד יו"ד מן יב"ק ונשאר קב כו': **ב. ויתפלל אל ה'.**
על מזונו וחסרונו ויאמר: **הלא זה דברי עד היותי על אדמתי.** למה הרע לי ואם
לא שבתי שם גם אני רציתי לשוב אך שאמרתי שבזקנותי יום א' לפני מתתי
אשוב כי אתה מקבל תשובת השבים ביום אחד כמו שעשית להם אך שנטרפה
השעה ולא יכולתי לשוב עד בואו עד זמן עד היותי מוטל על אדמה: **ע"כ קדמתי**
לברוח תרשישה. שלכן קדמתי בנעורותי לברוח מלפניך כי חשבתי שבזקנותי
אשוב: **כי ידעתי כי אתה אל חנון ורחום ארך אפים.** שמארך אף להמתין אולי

ישוב ע"ז בטחתי אבל האו' אחטא ואשוב כו' ובאמת משפטי ה' אמת: **ורב חסד.**
שאתה מקבל אפי' ע"א לפני מותו: וע"כ תרחם עלי עכשיו: **ונחם על הרעה.**

ג. ועתה ה' קח נא את נפשי ממני. אם א"א להציל מרעתי כמ"ש במעשה דר"א
בן פדת (בפ"ג דתענית) דא"ל השי"ת בני ניחא לך דאחרבינן לעלמא כו' ואמרו
בזוהר שימו' ר"א כו' ע"ש וגם ר"ש שאל שני דחיי דחיינא או דחיינא ואם לאו הי'
גם רצונו בכך: **כי טוב מותי מחיי.** כמ"ש ושבח אני את המתים שכבר מתו מן
החיים אשר הם חיים כו' ולכאורה שכבר מתו וכן אשר הם חיים ייתור דברים
אלא שר"ל שטובים מן המתים שכבר מתו ולא נצטרכו לבא בגלגול מאותן שהם
חיי' עדנא שבאו בגלגול. ובזה מיושב דאמרו בערובין (פ"ק) נמנו וגמרו טוב
לאדם שלא נברא כו' עד יפשפש במעשיו דקשה האיך אפי' ה"ל שטוב יותר א"כ
למה נברא ועוד שעכשיו שנברא קשה להולמו. ועוד מאי יפשפש כו' הל"ל יעבוד
את ד' ויעשה טוב אלא נראה דנחלקו בשוב אל הגלגול שני. שאלו אומרים טוב
לו שנברא כי בכל פעם הוא עושה מצות כמ"ש קצת מפרשים. ואלו אומרים טוב
לו יותר אם הי' מתקן בגלגול ראשון ולא יצטרך בגלגול שני. וכן נמנו וגמרו כנ"ל
וזהו ושבח אני את המתים כו' וקאמרי ועכשיו שנברא ע"כ לתקן מעשיו שמקודם
ולא בשביל מצוה לעשות כי טוב לו כו' וע"כ כנ"ל וע"כ יראה עיקר לתקן במה שפשע
מקדם כמ"ש אבוך במאי זהיר טפי כו' והאיך ידע מה שקלקל מקדם יש ע"ז ב'
סימנים א' במה שנכשל בה בגלגול הזה הרבה פעמים. וע"ז אמרו יפשפש
במעשיו באיזה נכשל ב' באיזה עבירה נפשו חשקה לו מאד לפי שהורגלה מקודם
ונעשה טבע ולכך, יש ב"א שחושקין בעבירה אחת יותר וזה בעבירה אחרת וע"ז
אמרו יפשפש במעשיו שיפשפש את מעשיו: **ד. ויאמר ה' ההיטב כו'.** וכי הדבר
הזה טוב אתה עושה שחרה לך ואתה מקנא בהם כמו למה חרה לך אצל קין: **ה.**
ויצא יונה מן העיר. כי ראה שהשם לא שמע תפלתו והשעה דחוקה לו פירש
עצמו מן העוה"ז: **וישב מקדם לעיר.** שישב לעסוק בתורה שהיא נבראת קודם
עוה"ז כמ"ש ה' קנני כו' קדם מפעליו מאז: **ויעש לו שם סוכה וישב תחתיה**
בצל. כמ"ש באספך כו' תחוגו את חג כו' בסוכות כו' ואמרו בפסולות גורן ויקב
כו' ואמרו שיהא צלתה מרובה מחמתה. והענין כי כל מעשה עוה"ז ועשרו וטובו
הכל מן השמש והוא שאמרו במזלא תליא מלתא כפי אשר השמש עומדת
במזלות והוא ידוע להחוזים ולכך כתבה התורה באספך כו' שלא תמשך אחר
העוה"ז תעשה סוכה בפסולות גורן ויקב שכל סעודה הוא על הלחם ויין כמ"ש
(קהלת י') לשחוק עושים לחם ויין כו' ואמרו שלא תהנה מהן אלא בפסולות
ותפרוש מעושר מעושר עוה"ז רק תשב בצל שלא תחת השמש ויהי תורתך קבע
ומלאכתך ארעי וזהו צלתה מרובה מחמתה וזהו וישב בצל ולא עסק כלום עד
אשר יראה מה יהיה מן מזלו אם ישונה לטובה וצפה תמיד אולי ישונה וחפץ ה'
להראותו שאין טובת עוה"ז כלום: **ו. וימן ה' אלהים קיקיון.** כי אותם שמזלם
קשה והן דוחקים את השעה וא"י שישנה ה' את המזל כמ"ש שכינה לר"א בן
פדת דניחא לך דאחרבי לעלמא כו' ונוטל ה' מחלקו בג"ע ונותן לו בעוה"ז
כמעשה דר"א בן פדת וכן ברבה בר אבוה שלקח מטרפי דג"ע והענין שכל עושר
עוה"ז הוא מטרפי אילנא דג"ע וכמ"ש בזווהר וזהו וימן ה' כו' שנתן לו עושר גדול

מעלי ג"ע: **ויעל מעל ליונה להיות צל על ראשו.** כי השמש מכה אותו שנולד בחסרון כי כל טוב ורע הכל מהשמש הואיל והכל תחת השמש בין טוב ובין רע התחיל לגלות כי הכל יאבד כשם שהשמש נותן כך נוטלת ממנו ונותנת לאחר כמ"ש וזרח השמש ובא השמש שנוטל מזה ונותן לזה וז"א וזרח השמש את מזלו ואח"כ ובא השמש אל מקומו שואף אל מקום המוכן לאחר ליתן זורח הוא שם לכך נתן לו הקיקיון לצל על ראשו להציל אותו מהשמש: **להציל לו מרעתו.** להציל אותו מצרותיו ודוחקיו: **וישמח יונה על הקיקיון שמחה גדולה.** ששמח מאוד שהגיע אל תאותו וזה אמרם (בשבת כ"א) ארבע"ח לדידי חזי קיקיון דיונה כו' עד בריחי דמערבא. וג"ל שזה כוונתו שהוא ראה עושר גדול ויצלוליבא דמי לאילן סרק שאין עושה פירות כלל. ומדפסקי רב' בין בצעי המים בני אדם שאינם מהוגנים כמ"ש ביחזקאל (ל"ד) ומשקע מים תשתו ואת הנותרים ברגליכם תרפשון. ועל פום חנותא מדלן יתה כמ"ש החנות פתוחה וכל הרוצה כו'. ומפרצדוהי עבדה משחא של פעמים מוכן לזרעם שיטיבו בה כמ"ש (פסחים דף מ"ט) זמנין דנפיק ברא מעלי מיני' ואכיל לי' ומקיים בו מה שנאמר (איוב כ"ז) יכין וצדיק ילבש זרע מעליא. ובענפוהי נייחין שהם מחזיקין ידי ת"ח כמ"ש בב"ב כל בריחי הן הת"י כמ"ש בר"ה מאן קצירי מריע ת"ח דמערבא כי עתירי בבל אמרו יורדי כו' כמ"ש בב"ב ע"ש. ז) **וימן האלהים תולעת בעלות השחר למחרת.** כמ"ש כי בכל עלות השחר עומדת קליפה א' שרוצה ליטול את כל השפע ונקרא תולע והוא נגד שם ראשון של מ"ב שהוא בבוקר מדרש של אברהם כידוע לי"ח. וע"ז באה עולת תמיד עולת נגד תולע וזה אמרו **ותך את הקיקיון וייבש.** שנטל עשרו להודיע כי טובת עוה"ז אין. ח) **ויהי כזרוח השמש.** אחר שהוסר ממנו זרחה עליו השמש כמקודם בחסרונו וימן אלהים רוח קדים. מהשמש והוא אותו רוח שהי' עליו. חרשית כמ"ש נאלמתי דומיה החשתי מטוב כו' כ"פ מתורה ועשרו לא עמדה לו ונשאר קרח מכאן וקרח מכאן: **ותך השמש על ראש יונה ויתעלף.** שהכה אותו רוע מזלו מאוד כמ"ש שחורה אני ונאוה כו' אע"פ שאני שחורה ברוע מזלי מ"מ אני נאוה במעשי כו' אל תראוני שאני שחרחורת ששזפתני השמש כנ"ל. בני אמי הוא הגוף הראשון ששניהם מאם א' מן האדמה. נחרו בי היא יבשם אותו שמוני כו' שפנה אל העוה"ז לטרוח בעד העולם שאינו עולם שלו כמ"ש כי ישבעו זרים כוחך. כרמי שלי כו' עולם שלי עוה"ב לא נטרתי לכך אני שחורה עכשיו: **וישאל את נפשו למות ויאמר טוב מותי מחיי.** כנ"ל כמ"ש כיון שמריעין לא במהרה כו': ט. **ויאמר אלהים אל יונה ההיטב חרה לך אל הקיקיון.** על ממון של הבל. כמ"ש (יומא דף ע"א) ושנות חיים כו' אלו שנותיו של אדם שמתהפכין לו מרעה לטובה ועכשיו שניטל ממנו נפרד ממנו החיים: י. **ויאמר ה' אתה חסת על הקיקיון אשר לא עמלת בו ולא גדלתו.** שלא עסקת במ"ע ולא ביגיע כפיך וגם לא הי' אתך זמן רב שתשמור אותו: **שבין לילה היה ובין לילה אבד.** שהעושר אינו לאדם אלא בעוה"ז שדומה ללילה: יא. **ואני לא אחוס על נינוה העיר הגדולה.** על העוה"ז ובפרט על המאמינים בי ולכך נקראת העולם עיר הגדולה ע"ש הגדולה בעוה"ז: **אשר יש בה הרבה משתים עשרה רבוא אדם.** כי

התי״ח נקרא אדם כנ״ל וכתיב האלף לך שלמה וכו׳ ופי׳ מהרש״א (בשבועות דף ל״ה) שמן אלף שהוא כולם לה׳ שהכל לו מאתים לנוטרים את פריו שהם התי״ח זהו מדבריו המגע לדברינו א״כ מס׳ רבוא הן י״ב רבוא. רק שיש פרוטרוט יותר מס׳ רבוא הוא ולכך אמר ית׳ אשר יש בה הרבה כו׳ אע״פ שהגמרא קאמר (שם) אמר שמואל מלכותא דקטיל א׳ משיתא בעלמא לא מיענשא שנאמר האלף לך שלמה ומאתים לנוטרים את פריו למלכותא דארעא חשב מלגאו ופשטי׳ דקרא מלבר כמו (ויקרא כ״ב) ואיש כי יאכל קדש בשגגה: **אשר לא ידע בין ימינו לשמאלו.** ששתי כליות יועצות כו׳ א׳ לטובה כו׳ שנאמר לב חכם כו׳ אבל הצדיק עובד ה׳ בשתיהן כמ״ש בכל לבבך בשני יצריך כו׳ ולא ידע ההפרש בין ימינו לשמאלו: **ובהמה רבה.** שאר ב״א כמ״ש אדם ובהמה תושיע ה׳:

בריך רחמנא דסייען מרישא ועד כאן

This volume is part of
THE ARTSCROLLSERIES®
an ongoing project of
translations, commentaries and expositions
on Scripture, Mishnah, Talmud, Halachah,
liturgy, history, the classic Rabbinic writings,
biographies, and thought.

For a brochure of current publications
visit your local Hebrew bookseller
or contact the publisher:

Mesorah Publications, ltd

4401 Second Avenue
Brooklyn, New York 11232
(718) 921-9000